# Jim Britt's

# Cracking the Rich Code$^3$

Inspiring Stories, Insights and Strategies from Entrepreneurs Around the World

STAY IN TOUCH WITH JIM AND KEVIN

For daily strategies and insights from top entrepreneurs, join us at

THE RICH CODE CLUB

**FREE** members site.

www.TheRichCodeClub.com

Cracking the Rich Code$^3$

Jim Britt



Cracking the Rich Code, LLC

10556 Combie Road, Suite 6205

Auburn, CA 95602



Jim Britt

Cracking the Rich Code$^3$

ISBN: 978-1-64153-305-8

**Co-authors from Around the World**


Jim Britt

Kevin Harrington

Dr. Tom Heemstra

Amy Oppedisano

Shirlene Reeves

Colleen Duggan

Vishal Bajpai

Kate Miller

Evans Duren

Sara Plinska Camilo

James Hyde

Shanda Gobeli

Zahra Karsan

Evan Sanchez

Dr. Spencer Holman

Shahnaz Ghafoor

Karin Lubin

Chris Baniewicz

Matthew Hardy

Rory Douglas

Terry L Perez

Dr. Tianna Conte

# DEDICATION

*Entrepreneurs will change the world.*

*They always have and they always will.*

*To the entrepreneurial spirit that lives within each of us.*

# Foreword by Kevin Harrington

You probably know me as one of the “Sharks” on the hit TV show Shark Tank, where I was an investor in many entrepreneurial ventures.

But my life and business wasn't always like that. I used to be your regular, everyday

guy patching cracked driveways to make money. I had hopes and dreams just like most, yet I worked around people who didn't support my dreams. But you know what? I not only found a way out, but I found a way to my dreams... and so can you.

Now, I wake up every morning excited about my day, and I surround with only the people I want in my life; entrepreneurs who really want something more than just getting by paycheck to paycheck.

Today we hear stories -- mostly from the mainstream media -- everyday about how bad things are, businesses are closing and jobs being lost, interest rates are on the rise, how the gap between rich and poor is growing and how you'll never make it on your own.

But here's what I know for sure. Entrepreneurs are going to change the world. We always have and we always will.

Forget the 1% vs the 99%. 100% of us entrepreneurs need answers. We need solutions. We need something more than what we're being told by those who don’t have a clue. We need to start saying Yes! to opportunity and No! to all the noise.

The fact is that it's a new world and a new economy. The "proven" methods of doing business and investing that produced successful results, even two years ago, simply may not work anymore.

If you want to succeed (or even survive) in our new world, you need an entirely new set of skills and information.

You need to "reposition" yourself…often.

You need to revamp how you do business…often.

You need to change how you handle and invest your money…often.

Like any other situation, if you know WHAT to do and WHEN to do it, you'll not only be "safe"... you could easily skyrocket financially.

If you have the right knowledge for today, the right opportunities for today, the right strategies for today and most of all the right character and mindset for today, you can win — and you can win big!

What I've discovered in my over three-decade career as an entrepreneur, is that success in the face of financial adversity boils down to 3 things:

The right knowledge at the right time.

The right opportunities at the right time.

The right you... ALL the time.

The bottom line is this: you can no longer afford to rely on anyone else to navigate your financial future. You have to rely on your "self." The question is... do you have a "self" you can rely on? Unfortunately, when it comes to entrepreneurship and money, many people don't. They don't have the financial education, the mental toughness, the knowledge and the skills to build wealth... especially in an ever-changing marketplace. You need to get RE-educated. You need to REINVENT yourself for success in the new economy. You need to learn new strategies in the areas of business and career, finance and real estate that create wealth or at least financial freedom in today's new world. But that's not all...

Skills and strategies and all that profound new knowledge won't do you one bit of good if you don't have the CHARACTER, the HABITS and the MENTALITY it takes to get rich. If you have internal barriers, your road to success will be slow and full of pain and struggle. It's like driving with one foot on the gas and one foot on the brake and always wondering why you aren't getting anywhere. Your mind is working against you instead of for you.

I have seen business owners come to me with their business ready to go under — and have the next year be their best financial year ever. I've see others that had a business that should skyrocket, yet fail because they didn't have the mental toughness to go the distance. I have seen people stuck in dead-end, dreary jobs break out of their rut, get involved in a brand-new passion, and become wildly successful.

No matter what you do for a living...regardless of your education, level of business experience or current financial status…If you have a burning desire for financial change then you won't want to miss this rare opportunity to learn from the entrepreneurs within this book.

It will provide you with some of the same success strategies that Jim Britt and I have used personally and shared with tens of thousands of people who've had tremendous financial success…people just like you, who wanted to get out of the rat race and enjoy financial freedom.

In addition, you'll learn what others have done, mistakes they made and how you can avoid them. You'll discover strategies that could make your business into a major market leader. I always say, "Just one good idea can change everything."

Success is predictable if you know what determines it. This book offers some valuable tips, knowledge, insights, skill sets, that will challenge you to leap beyond your current comfort level. If you want to strengthen your life, your business and your effectiveness overall, you'll discover a great friend in this book. You'll probably want to recommend it to all your entrepreneurial friends.

Although I haven't followed Jim Britt's career over the last 40 years, but I do know that he is recognized as one of the top thought leaders in the world, helping millions of people create prosperous lives. He has authored 13 books and multiple programs showing people how to understand their hidden abilities to do more, become more and enjoy more in every area of life. I also want to recognize Joel Sauceda, our online business partner. He is the brains behind the many online PR, Marketing, Branding and Lead Generation strategies each entrepreneur coauthor and reader of the book will benefit from.

The principles, concepts and ideas within this book are sometimes simple, but can be profound to a person who is ready for that perfect message at the right time and is willing to take action to change.

Maybe for one it's a chapter on leadership or mindset. For the next, it's a chapter on raising capital, or securing a business loan. Each chapter is like opening a surprise empowering gift.

The conclusion to me is an exciting one. You, me and every other human being are shaping our brains and bodies by our attitude, the decisions we make, the intentions we hold and the actions we take daily. Why is it exciting? Because we are in control of all these things and we can change as long as we have the intention, willingness and commitment to look inside, take charge of our lives and make the changes.

I want to congratulate Jim Britt for making this publication series available and for allowing me to write the foreword, a chapter in each book and be involved with the entrepreneurs within this book and series. I honor Jim and the coauthors within this book and the series for the lives they are changing.

As you enter these pages, do so slowly and with an open mind. Savor the wisdom you discover here, and then with interest and curiosity discover what rings true for you, and then take action toward the life you want.

So many people settle for less in life, but I can tell you from my experience that it doesn't have to be that way.

Be prepared…because your life and business, is about to change!

Jim Britt & Kevin Harrington

As co-creators of this book series Jim Britt and Kevin Harrington have devoted their lives to helping others to live a more prosperous, fulfilled and happy life. Over the years they have influenced millions of lives through their coaching, mentoring, business strategies and leading by example. They are committed to never ending self-improvement and an inspiration to all they touch. They are both a true example that all things are possible. If you get a chance to work with Kevin and Jim or becoming a coauthor in a future Cracking the Rich Code book, jump at the chance!

# Table of Contents

# Jim Britt

Jim Britt is an internationally recognized leader in the field of peak performance and personal empowerment training. He is author of 13 best-selling books, including *Rings of Truth; The Power of Letting Go; Freedom; Unleashing Your Authentic Power; Do This. Get Rich-For Entrepreneurs; The Flaw in The Law of Attraction;* and *The Law of Realization,* to name a few. He is the creator of a collaborative book series for entrepreneurs *Cracking the Rich Code.*

Jim has presented seminars throughout the world sharing his success principles and life-enhancing realizations with thousands of audiences, totaling over 1,500,000 people from all walks of life.

Jim has served as a success counselor to over 300 corporations worldwide. He was recently named as one of the world's top 20 success coaches, top 50 speakers and presented with the best of the best award out of the top 100 contributors of all time to the direct selling industry.

As an entrepreneur, Jim has launch 28 business ventures in the past 40 years and knows how to guide beginning and seasoned entrepreneurs toward a successful venture and avoid the classic mistakes made by the majority of new business launches.

Jim is more than aware of the challenges we all face in making adaptive changes for a sustainable future.

## There is Power in Letting Go

### *By Jim Britt*

Imagine walking into a room where groups of people are seated at a table where a succulent meal was set before them. Their table is filled with every sort of food you can imagine. It's a mouth-watering display, all perfectly prepared and it's all right in front of their noses and easily within their reach.

You notice however, that none of these people are eating. They haven't even taken a single bite. Their plates are empty, and it appears that they have been seated there for a very long time, so long that they appear to be starving to death.

They are starving, not because they cannot see or eat all the food before them, or because eating it is forbidden or harmful. They aren't eating because they don't realize that food is what they need. They don't know that those very sharp pains in their stomachs are caused by hunger. They don't see that all they need to do to stop their suffering is to eat the food that's right in front of them.

This is an example of our basic human suffering as well. Most of us sense that there is something wrong, that something that is inherently missing in our lives, but we haven't a clue how to overcome the problem. We may have an inkling that what we need is somehow very close to us, but we don't connect the lack of it to the sharp pain inside us. With time, as the pain becomes even more severe, we start to believe that being in pain is just a normal part of living.

About 35 years ago I kept noticing that so many people feel stuck. And as hard as they tried to break free, they kept ending up in the same place over and over again. Sort of like an exciting ride on a roller coaster that drops you off at the same place you started.

I started thinking about the habit patterns we develop that are beneficial to everyday life, like driving a car, for example. After we do it for a while it becomes second nature. We no longer think about how to drive a car, we just get in and go. If that's true, and it is, then our negative habits can also become second nature. We get stuck in a habit pattern and we can't figure out why we keep repeating the same results over and over.

An example, I was speaking with a man the other day and he shared with me that he had not been able to fully pay his bills every month, for over 25 years! His habit pattern has become so second nature to him that he can't even see it. After a while it becomes a core belief that he can never pay his bills on time. And you will do almost anything to prove to yourself and the outside world, that what you believe it true…even to your determent. It's like an addiction.

Let's say you are feeling the pain of unhappiness. You suffer from it daily, unaware that you can eliminate your suffering and find happiness by simply making the right choices and by letting go of those habit patterns holding you back. The problem is that our emotional conflicts are so familiar to us that they keep us blinded to better possibilities. We actually become addicted to feeling the way we do, thinking that it is just the way things are and we resign ourselves to getting by and coping.

The million-dollar question for a lot of people is how do we let go and walk away from what's familiar to us? How do we let go of our pain and conflicts? I believe that most people have a desire to do more with their lives, to be happy, to be financially successful, and not suffer their emotional pains, but most often their fear of taking risks and the pain of change prevents them from even trying. We very often fear what we want most. And at the same time, we get what we fear most. Our mental programming is so averse to risk that it prefers to keep us safe and secure within the status quo, so we stay where we are even though we are miserable. Just look around you. You see it everywhere. If most people want to be happy and successful, what is it that keeps them from making the changes they need to make to get there? People say they want to change but do they really?

Do a little exercise. Do you feel that you are more successful now than five years ago? Have you truly made significant progress? Have the last five years turned out the way you wanted them to be? And if not, why not?

When you break free from the patterns of the past and you begin to see the truth behind the conflict watch what happens to your life.

What will happen is that the people, experiences and opportunities will begin to flow to you. You'll begin to see conflict as just a mental and emotional mistake. Letting go of conflict is a choice. When faced with a conflict, ask yourself this very important question. "What benefit am I getting from holding on to this conflict? Does it serve my higher good? Am I willing to trade an abundant life for hanging onto something that doesn't serve my higher good? Am I willing to spend my vital energy for something that doesn't take me in the direction I want to go?

Many experts say just face your fears, do the thing you fear most and the fear will go away. Well, that's easy to say and even makes sense when you hear it. But how about all the people who are afraid to face their fears, too afraid to take the first step? What do they do? What about that buried feeling attached to the fear, what happens to that?

Let's face it. Life is risky. Going into business is risky. Getting married is risky…snow skiing, mountain climbing, driving past the speed limit, raising children is risky…I could go on and on. All these activities are risky, but we choose to do them anyway, don't we?

Let's first gain an understanding of the true definition of fear. "Fear is taking a past experience, projecting it into the future, with the anticipation of it happening again, and then re-living it in the moment." Fear is simply trapped energy you hold inside that was created from a past traumatic experience, or series of experiences over time. Fear is a mental mistake. It's a made-up story. It's friction in your thought process. When you get hurt emotionally you feel the pain inside. Then you hold onto that painful experience hoping that it will protect you from it happening again, but it won't.

Fear is simply trapped energy wanting to be released. And once you gain that understanding it becomes easier to let it go of the fear.

Look at it this way. Every action you take is either based in fear or love. If you move toward what you love, you naturally move away from what you fear. While you are moving toward what you love and you feel the fear, face it yes, but do more than that. Observe it. Separate yourself from it and see it for what it is, which is just a made-up story, a mental mistake. It's your subconscious programming bringing it up saying "Hey, do you need this anymore or would you like to delete it?" Your fear is NOT you. It's just a passenger you have picked up along the way. It is not hanging onto you, instead you are hanging on to it!

When a fear feeling surfaces, breathe into it and when you exhale, let it go. Then take a course of action that will bring you more of what you love. Just the fact that you have observed yourself feeling the fear, and you see it for what it really is, you have weakened its hold on you…or rather your hold on it.

Letting go is a choice, moment to moment. It's a fork in the road. It's a choice to buy into the delusion of our mind chatter, of past pains and programming, or move toward what you would love to have in your life.

If you want to increase your level of productivity, once you have decided what you want to accomplish, ask yourself moment to moment, "Is this action I am taking moving me toward my desired outcome or further away. Success at anything is that simple.

Whatever happened to you in the past is not happening to you now unless you let it. The past is only your story and it's not real today. It's a memory, a trapped energy pattern. It's like an old movie that you just keep watching over and over, until you decide you've watched it enough.

What's real is the stress headache, anxiety, the lack of success and unhappiness you've created for yourself out of something that doesn't exist any longer. That's what's real. Think about it.

Any sort of permanent change, whether it be losing weight, quitting smoking, getting healthier, earning more money, having a more fulfilling relationship, or breaking an emotional addictive cycle, to eventually be free of it requires several things.

The first thing required is a desire to change. You have to want something bad enough in order to make any permanent change. Desire has to come from inside you. No one else can create that for you. I'm assuming that you have a desire to change otherwise you wouldn't be reading this book.

The next step is that you must make a decision to change. It's not important that you know how to change at this point, but it is important that you have made a firm decision to change. A decision to do one thing eliminates something else. For example, if you want to be wealthy, you have to first make a decision to "be" a wealthy person. Once that decision is made that eliminates the decision to do anything less. You can't have the mindset of a wealthy person and one that can't pay his bills every month. You can't make both decisions at the same time. You might say, "Well I am working on developing a wealth mindset." Well, if that's the case, you have chosen to be the person that can't pay his bills monthly. You are one or the other…fat or skinny, healthy or non-healthy, wealthy or not, drug user or not. Whatever it is you want is not a decision to "give it a try," but a decision to do it!

The next step is taking action toward what you want. When you do, again, you must realize that every action you take from this point forward is either moving you in the direction of your desired outcome or away from it. There is no middle ground. We live in a black and white world, not a gray world. You want to lose weight, but you still stop at a fast food place for lunch, simple means you need to re-evaluate your decision. There is no right and wrong here. It just is what it is.

In order to get something different in your life, you must do something in a different way, and that will require you stepping out of your comfort zone. Anything, anything you want lies just one step in the right direction…just taking one small step, one possible uncomfortable step at a time until you reach your desired outcome.

When you take steps to change, you'll always be faced with discomfort, fears and doubt. In fact, changing can bring up your deepest fears…fears of failing…what if I can't do this? What if it doesn't work? What will others think of me if I fail? I tried before and failed. What if I can't do it this time? The list goes on and on. It can even bring up the fear of success…what if I'm successful? Will I have to change? Can I handle the change? Will I be okay without this crutch? And, trust me, suffering, misery and conflict are all crutches that you'll remain attached to for life unless you decide to let them go and do something in a different way than you've done in the past. Change requires that you change. It's a battle between the old you and the new you, you want to become.

To overcome seemingly insurmountable obstacles, you have to be willing to endure some pain of change and along with that you have to be bold. You have to stand by your decision and not let the mind chatter pull you down. Change can be like free falling out of an airplane…it's both exhilarating and scary at the same time. You have to be so determined that you will let nothing throw you off course.

Remember that the "you" that is reading this book can't accomplish those things you want. In order to have those things you have to become a different "you." If you attempt to change using the same old thoughts and behaviors that you've always used, you'll end up with the same old results. Every income, and every life level, requires a different you.

Whatever you're feeling…depression, anger, fear or anxiety, remember as it comes up, that it is just energy wanting to be released and that you are in complete control. As you feel it, stop for a moment and observe your feeling and then ask yourself these questions.

"Do I like feeling this way?" If your answer is "no" move to the next question.

"Will honoring this feeling take me in the direction I want to go?" If your answer is "no" move to the next question.

"Do I want to let it go?" If your answer is "yes" move to the next question.

"Am I willing to let it go?" If your answer is "yes" then move to the last question.

"When…When will I let it go?"

And your answer should be apparent…NOW!

By the time you get to the last question you'll discover that the feeling has left you. It may come back, but you have advanced to the next level. With each release the feelings get weaker and less frequent.

Hanging on requires a tremendous amount of energy, sometimes all your energy, and it will get you nowhere except backwards to more of the same. Letting go, on the other hand, requires no energy at all. It's simply a choice!

The most important thing is to love yourself above all. Even falling in love with what you want to accomplish in life. The only other option is to fall in fear with it.

Any feeling that is not loving toward yourself or what you want to accomplish is based in fear. Darkness is the absence of light, just like fear is the "feeling" of the absence of love.

One of the most basic fears we have about letting go, is the fear of the emptiness we believe will be there when we do. But in reality, when you die to the old, a vacuum is created for the new.

That empty space is instantly filled with passion, new ideas and opportunities. When you simply surrender a fear, the vacuum is then filled with what you need to fulfill your dreams and ambitions.

If you become an observer of your emotions…really observe them, you will no longer be attached to them or controlled by them. You can just allow them to "be there" without acting on them. With practice, you will eventually come to the realization that the origin of suffering can be put aside and can be let go of.

Letting go simply means that you leave emotions as they are. Whatever you pay attention to grows in strength. What you don't pay attention to withers away from lack of attention. It does not mean that they are gone forever, even though some will be. It is more like observing and letting them be. Through the practice of letting go you'll begin to realize that hanging on to outdated experiences, feelings and emotions is the origin of suffering and conflict. You'll realize that all conflict is self-conflict.

When you find yourself attached, look at it this way. If you are holding onto this book and you set it down on the table, you have let it go. Just because you have the book in your hand doesn't mean you have to carry it with you day after day for the rest of your life. The book is not the problem, just like the emotional suffering is not the problem. The problem is hanging on to it. So, what do you do? Let it go, lay it aside. You simply put it down gently without any kind of conflict, just like putting the book on the table and walking away.

Now, this doesn't mean you don't handle any problems that arise. Handle your problems, yes, but do it without the emotional attachment.

You can apply this insight to letting go of fear, anger, anxiety or any other self-conflict. So, when you are feeling inner conflict, the moment that you refuse to indulge in that feeling, you are letting go, and you are in control.

We all have moments when everything we do just seems to work. It is during these times that great insights occur. We feel abundant, happy and trusting of life. We are refreshingly still inside, our usual nagging "chatter" is quiet, and our energy flow is profoundly open. In this state we are able to experience our own true nature, love, passion, productivity, and the full beauty of our surroundings. We feel alive, balanced and purposeful. Then suddenly, without any notice at all, this vibrant, loving state disappears as mysteriously as it came. Our soaring spirit seems to fall back to sleep, as we drift back into our old identity. We begin to once again "buy into" the illusionary, self-created tensions of worry, fear, depression, anxiety and scarcity, which restrict us from being in the moment and living the life we want.

Remember that any feeling that is not taking you where you want to go is based in fear. When you let go of fear all you have left is that empty space that can be filled with the answers you seek. Letting go leaves you with that feeling you had when you first fell in love. Love is an energy that travels so fast that it's everywhere at once. Even in your darkest moments love is always present, when you let go of what you fear. In fact, it's love presenting you with the fear saying "If you let go of this, you can have more of me."

We have some misconceptions about love, however. The first is that it comes from outside us, and the second, is that it is secured through relationships. If we narrow love down to these two things, we are cheating ourselves out of the endless possibilities that exist. Love is always present inside us. It's just that we've disconnected by buying into our fears.

The depth of connection you feel becomes stronger as you let go of the fear, doubt, anger, blame, etc. Love is the spirit that lives within each of us. It's where all things originate.

Once you begin the process of letting go you see that every seemingly painful event is truly a gift designed to show us the power of love, if we'll just let go and embrace it. Remember: What you pursue will always elude you. What you become is what you'll create. If you pursue love, it will always be "out there" somewhere, in the next relationship, job, success or outside event. When you love yourself, you'll begin to discover love in everything we do, and in everyone you meet.

Receiving comes first, then giving. And what you give to others, you also give to yourself.

And of course, the reverse is also true: What you withhold from yourself, you withhold from others, and again from yourself.

Letting go is essential in living a balanced life. Too much focus in one area of your life can literally suck the energy and life out of another area. When you are in balance energy flows as it should, and so does your success and happiness.

***

To contact Jim:

www.JimBritt.com

www.JimBrittCoaching.com

www.LiveLifeAtLevelTen.com

www.TheRichCodeClub.com

www.RichCode.club

www.PowerOfLettingGo.com

www.FaceBook.com/JimBrittOnline

www.linkedin.com/in/jim-britt

# Kevin Harrington

Kevin Harrington is an original shark from the hit TV show *Shark Tank* and a successful entrepreneur for more than forty years. He's the co-founding board member of the Entrepreneurs' Organization and co-founder of the Electronic Retailing Association. He also invented the infomercial. He helped make "But wait... There's more!" part of our cultural history. He's one of the pioneers behind the *As Seen on TV* brand, has heard more than 50,000 pitches, and launched more than 500 products generating more than $5 Billion in global sales. Twenty of his companies have generated more than $100 million in revenue each. He's also the founder of the *Secrets of Closing the Sale Master Class* inspired by the Master of sales—Zig Ziglar. He's the author of several bestselling books including *Act Now: How I Turn Ideas into Million Dollar Products, Key Person of Influence,* and *Put a Shark in Your Tank.*

## Becoming A KPI

***By Kevin Harrington***

The Key Person of Influence (KPI) in any given industry is the leader. It is the leader of the business world, the leader of automobile dealerships, the leader of selling hats—you name it. In other words, being the KPI means being the go-to person. The crazy thing? Anyone can be a Key Person of Influence. Any entrepreneur can be a KPI, a doctor, a salesperson, anyone. Just follow five steps and you will be well on your way. What comes with being a Key Person of Influence is value, ideally a massive amount of money, and being the leader in your field. The KPI is the person who comes up in conversations when it relates to a certain product, business, company, industry, or field. This is the person others seek out, the go-to person. Being the Key Person of Influence is how I got on *Shark Tank.*

Here's the story: I got a phone call from Mark Burnett's company. Mark Burnett is a television producer. He produced shows like *Survivor* and *The Voice*. His office called to set up an appointment. Mark was starting up a new show and wanted me to go out to Los Angeles to talk business. I was curious as to how Mark Burnett's company found me, and why they reached out for my services. They told me it was because I was a Key Person of Influence. I was all over the internet as a result of everything I was doing. It was 2008, and I had been in the business for 25 years. I had created huge brands. I helped build Tony Little. I helped build Jack Lalanne. I helped build Food Saver. We did the NuWave Oven. We worked with people like George Foreman and countless others. The problem was, everybody knew the brands, which was good for business, but did nothing for my personal brand. Consumers knew about the Food Saver, they knew about Tony Little, and they knew about Jack Lalanne, but not everyone knew I was the guy behind all of these people. Nobody knew me.

At that point, I made a conscious effort to build my brand. I wanted to become the go-to person so I could get the hot products and the phone calls. I helped build Tony Little's business, but everyone called him; they weren't calling me. What's wrong with that picture? Well, for one, I invested millions and millions of dollars of my own capital into Tony Little, and then he got all the phone calls. Shame on me for doing that, right? So, I decided to build my brand, and that's when I came out with my book, *Key Person of Influence*. I promoted myself by doing radio talk shows, TV shows, trade journals, speeches, etc. This is how I got on *Shark Tank*.

If I hadn't met Daniel Priestley, my book could have become *How To Become The Go-To Guy* because that's what I was looking to do, but Daniel very eloquently created this five-step system called the "Key Person of Influence." Realizing we were on to something, we co-authored and launched *Key Person of Influence*. Let's look now at the necessary steps to become a KPI.

**Obtaining Customers**

In 1984, I started a business of obtaining customers on TV. One evening, I was watching the Discovery Channel and suddenly the channel went dark for about six hours. I then called the cable company just in case there was a problem. They told me there wasn't a problem, that the Discovery Channel was an 18-hour network. That's when the light bulb went off. This was downtime. They put no value on those six down hours. Instead of showing something during this time, bars were put up on the screen. I started thinking about what I could put in place of that downtime, to sell something, obtain customers, and make money. I'm like the Rembrandt TV guy. I created and invented the whole concept of going to TV stations and buying huge blocks of remnant downtime. In all these years of me doing this, no one has challenged the idea that I was the person who did it, created it, and invented 30-minute infomercial blocks.

I was buying big blocks of time. Why? Because I wanted to obtain customers. How do you obtain customers? A lot of ways, but you ultimately have to get some form of media. How does it start? There are two metrics you have to look at when obtaining customers. What does it cost to obtain the customer? That is called the Cost Per Order (CPO). What is your Average Lifetime Revenue Value (ALRV), or Average Order Value (AOV)? The cost to obtain the customer obviously has to be less than the cost you are going to receive in income from the customer. The bottom line in obtaining customers: you have to set up a system. You have to set up testing. You have to set up as many sources for obtaining customers as possible. Even though I was in the TV business, I didn't just get customers through TV. Customers came through TV, radio, the internet, retail stores, international distribution, home shopping channels, etc. The first step is to make a laundry list of every possible resource for attracting these customers.

Today, some people who are into the digital space are basically just getting customers on the internet. Some of the areas I mentioned above have become very expensive. It's tougher to make money on TV. While we started on TV, the cost to get customers has become too high; so we now have made the switch to digital. When you talk about internet, there's many different ways to obtain customers, from Google AdWords to Facebook ads to social media, etc. You can also attain customers with public relations and influencers. You have to decide what works best with your product. The bottom line is a lot of people do not realize they have to be sophisticated, from a business analysis standpoint, to set up a business. You need a marketing plan to obtain customers.

First, focus on two numbers: your Customer Acquisition Cost (CAT) and Average Order Value (AOV). Those numbers have to work. Customer service is crucial in the business world as well. A business can't have bad customer service and retain customers This is especially true in this day-and-age.

**Raising Capital**

I had a 50-million-dollar-a-year business, making $5 million a year in profit. Feeling confident, I met with seven banks to get some financing. I thought it was going to be easy because I had a very profitable business. Unfortunately, bank after bank after bank turned me down. I had great credit and all of that. The only asset I had was the business. Part of the problem was I didn't know how to approach the banks. I was a young entrepreneur in my twenties. I had no real credibility in the banking world; I was walking in and just showing my numbers from the year before.

So, what did I do to get the capital? Well, I ran into a mentor who was a former bank president, and he said, "Kevin, you went about it all wrong. I come from the banking business, and if you walked into my office and said, 'I need 5 million bucks,' I would have told you to turn around and get the hell out of my office. What do you have to do? You have to sell them on the future. What you did last year is well and good, but they are giving you money because they know that you are still going to be in business three years from now repaying their loans. You need projections. You need your forward business plan. You need your five-year master plan. You need to talk the talk and walk the walk, otherwise they aren't even interested."

I hired my mentor as a consultant to the company. I brought him in on the ground floor as part of my dream team. To make a long story short, we went back to re-pitch some of the same banks. We didn't get 5 million dollars, but we got a 3-million-dollar line of credit. It was all in how we talked to the banks. We had the same business, but it was all in the presentation. It's all in how you talk and how prepared you are. Raising capital is mental. It's in the pitch. It's in the relationships you build, etc.

One of the biggest challenges with any business is having enough capital to do the things you want to do. You have to have a successful business plan if you want to raise money. Here are the elements of a successful business plan.

(1) You need an executive summary (one page summarizing the whole plan). You need an industry overview, defining the problem you are solving and an overview of the market.

(2) You need a description of your product or the service. How does it serve as a solution?

(3) You need a competitive analysis. What/who is your competition?

(4) You need a sales and marketing plan.

(5) You need to identify your target customer and proof for your concept.

(6) What is your method of operations?

(7) Who's on your management team, your board of advisers, your dream team?

(8) What are your financial projections?

(9) You need to outline your risk analysis and appendix.

If you are going to raise capital, you don't just talk to an investor. I get people all the time that come to me saying they have an idea, and boom… it's on a napkin. They tell me that they just need $100K for 10 percent. I ask if they can send me their business plan. They then ask me what I mean when I say, 'business plan.' If they don't have one, that means I am going to end up giving them 100K and never see it again.

One of the most important parts of raising capital is coming up with a reasonable ask, and then explaining how the proceeds will be used. Many entrepreneurs don't understand this. For example, a guy came on *Shark Tank* saying he needed 150K for 10 percent of his company. I asked what he was going to use the 150K for?

His response was essentially this, "Well, I am going to use the money as a down payment for a piece of real estate where we are going to build a building, then launch the business."

"Okay, so you are going to build the building and then equip the building with furniture. Where is that money going to come from?" I asked. He said once he got the real estate, then they would figure out that batch of money at that time. I told him, "$150K dollars doesn't get you in business. $150K dollars gets you a piece of land. How are you going to build the business, generate revenue, and pay me back?" This guy told me he thought I would have more money for him after that. I said, "Well, no. You are not going to get the first batch of money based on the answers you are giving me."

Instead, he should have said he was going to lease a small office and start generating massive amounts of revenue with the money I gave them. Then, pay me back all of my money, plus a huge return on my investment, and then build it into a global business. That's what I wanted to hear. I want to know that people have a successful business plan, a successful marketing plan, and then I will talk about how to go about raising the capital, how to call on investors, and what the sweet spots are for the investors.

The bottom line on raising capital is, you can't just go build yourself a huge global business without thinking about how you're going to finance it. In the old days, I thought if I built a successful business, money was going to be easy. It's not, unless you know how to do it.

There's an art to raising capital. Part of it involves making sure you are prepared and know how to pitch your business properly.

**The Perfect Pitch**

While the actual product or service you are trying to sell is a critical part of the process, it is just as important to sell the customer on yourself, your services, and your business. Even though I have made thousands upon thousands of pitches, have spoken to thousands of people, and have seen a great amount of success, I still pitch myself and my businesses. No matter who you are, or what you do, you have to be ready to drop the perfect pitch. It doesn't matter if you are going to make this perfect pitch in front of a crowd of thousands, or a crowd of one. To help with the concept of a perfect pitch, I have created a 10-step system.

Before you can start perfecting the perfect pitch, you have to ask yourself a couple of questions. What are you pitching? In other words, what product, business, or service are you trying to sell? Next, what do you want to get out of this pitch? More customers? More sales? Nonetheless, these questions are for you to answer, and you need to answer them before devising your perfect pitch. The perfect pitch can be broken down into these 10 steps:

**(1)** The **Tease** is your hook; the period of time when you plant the seed. This is when you reveal a problem. You have to explain to your customers why you are giving the pitch. You also have to use showmanship, which sets the pace for the rest of the pitch. If your showmanship skills are demonstrated in the Tease portion of your pitch, then you will have your audience (or your customer) hooked from the very beginning.

**(2)** Next up is **Please**. In this part of the perfect pitch, you are telling your customer how your product or service can solve the problem you mapped out in the first step. Ideally, your product or service will solve this stated problem in the most efficient, elegant, and cost-effective way. You have to relay to your customer that your solution is the best solution, and it will solve the problem better than anything (or anyone) else. It is important to also show off your features and benefits, and to display the magical transformation that will take place.

**(3)** The third step to the perfect pitch is **Demonstration/Multi-functionality**. First, you have to ask yourself if you can demonstrate your product, your service and your value. This is the key to any successful pitch, and it brings multi-functionality to the forefront. It shows it off. Think of this step as an added value. Ideally, your service or product is multifunctional. If you can show this off to your customer, then you just brought bonus points to the table.

**(4) But Wait There's More!** is the fourth step, and it's not just for infomercials on TV. This is the step where you give more value to your product or service by showing and adding more to the pitch—maybe added bonus items or "buy 2 get 1 free if you act now" incentives. At this point, your customer should already be biting, but now is the time to really win them over. So, show them what else you have to offer.

**(5) Testimonials** are the fifth step to creating the perfect pitch. You are now using someone else to do the pitching. In other words, who says so besides you? This is the proof behind your business, product, or service. Testimonials can include consumers (actual users of the product or service), professionals (leaders in your industry), editorial (articles, experts, press, journals, trade publications, magazines, newspapers), etc. Testimonials can also feature celebrities. Celebrity testimonials can be very powerful for the simple fact that people love celebrities. Then there are documented testimonials, which can include clinical studies, labs tests, and science. Once again, this is one of the most important areas for creating the perfect pitch.

**(6)** Another important step is **Research and Competitive Analysis**. For this step, you should be asking yourself if you have done your research. If so, then this is the portion of the perfect pitch when you show off all of that information. This can include information on the industry, market and competitors. It can also be facts, figures, and statistics. This research should show off the fact that you, your company, and your product/service is unique.

**(7)** The seventh step is **Your Team.** In this step, you are bringing the credibility of your team and putting it right there on the metaphorical table. Who makes up your team? It could be advisers, management, directors, and strategic partners. Your team will help scale, open connections, add on the knowledge factor, and so much more.

**(8) Why?** is the eighth step. Why are you pitching? How will the person in front of you help? This step will change based on who you are actually pitching to. For example, if you are looking for funds, then this is a big section, and you need to incorporate many talking points.

**(9)** The ninth step is **Marketing Plan.** You have done your pitch and given out all your information. Now, how will you make everything happen? For instance, you need to know your marketing and distribution plan. As is the case throughout your entire pitch, it is essential that you show confidence. Sell whoever you are pitching on your product or service, and yourself as well. People invest in people all the time.

**(10)** The 10th and final step is **Seize**. You laid everything out, now ask! What are you trying to accomplish? Ask it! Being the final step, this is the time to present the final call to action.

Remember, each pitch will be different. Some pitches last for over an hour and others last only a few seconds or minutes. It just depends on how much time you are given or how much time you need. That is why you need to craft your pitches accordingly. Practice, practice, and more practice.

***

To contact Kevin:

www.KevinHarrington.tv

# Dr Spencer J. Holman

Dr. Spencer J. Holman is a Philosopher, innovative thought leader, CEO of multiple successful companies, and internationally recognized author and speaker. His work is an integral part of universities, judicial systems, schools, churches and many other social environments around the world.

He is the creator of the 10 Life Values Philosophy, a personal and relational success system which serves as a blueprint for men to be equipped with processes and tools for success multi-generationally and inter-generationally. He has helped over 1 million men improve their lives, their families and their communities. His best-selling books include: Fatherhood Legacy, Fatherhood Academy, The Spiritual Guide, The Wealth Management Guide, and The Black Person's Guide to Owning A Bentley.

Dr. Holman has 4 Doctoral degrees: honorary PhD in Philosophy, of which his 10 Life Values success system is based, honorary Doctorate in Naturopathy, of which his herbal formulations and training series are founded. His honorary Doctorate in Community Development is based on his work of enlightening over 1 million men in the United States and across 26 countries internationally. His earned PhD in Theology encompasses his one-on-one and peer counseling, the creation of his Spiritual Guide and work as a Minister and Chaplain.

## The Value of The Rich Code: The American Dream

***By Dr. Spencer Holman***

What is your pursuit? From time immemorial we are conquerors seeking an inexplicable better way to go further in life. The American Dream symbolizes this pursuit. We are often lured into thinking that the individualistic path to success is more distinguished than the collectivist path; however, we would be better served to adopt the African proverb, "If you want to go quickly, go alone. If you want to go far, go together."

The American Dream is an ideology that represents a national ethos, the spirit of a country's culture, which captures and manifests the greatest of human aspirations and achievements. This ideology establishes and renews hope, that regardless of your plight in life or where you originated from, you can attain the most unimaginable life of success if you work hard, stay committed, and sacrifice. Often, the teachings of gurus, self-help books and success coaches leverage this belief, which is predicated on respecting humble beginnings, dreaming big, and being at the right place at the right time. Yet, getting rich has been evasive and elusive to the masses. Millions of people have gone into debt seeking the blueprint to success, but never grasped that the true secret to realizing your personal American Dream is understanding that every valued area of your life is a key component to cracking the code to riches.

Over twenty years ago, I created a value-based system, the 10 Life Values, that has consistently transformed people in their quest for acquiring and amassing personal riches. Across the United States and around the world, there are numerous stories of people who gained success and accumulated wealth in every area of their lives implementing my system. The distinctiveness and power of the 10 Life Values lie in its precision, yet pliable customization, which accommodates the randomness that stems from our choices, and the ever-shifting existence we call life. They offer a different set of lenses to view our whole world, breaking it down into 10 values: Spiritual, Health, Family, Appearance, Dwelling, Mobility, Education, Profession, Leisure and Wealth, and compartmentalizing them into distinct yet connected parts, which allow for greater focus and clarity in the areas best suited for the pursuit of our personal American Dream.

We nonchalantly use the concept of value, talk about value, being valued, doing things of value, treating others with value, or buying things of value, but rarely do we define what values are, what should be valued or how that value is determined. We should be exhausted by the researchers, data gatherers, and analyzers, who do not provide solutions or practical applications leading to purposeful actions. Values are beliefs and energy that perpetuate universal laws. They are transferred from one medium to another and motivate actions. Values indicate what we prioritize in our lives, what is important and held in high regard, and what is of great worth. Values are determined by 1) the influences around us in our environment, 2) messages we receive from our culture, and 3) our ability to understand, assimilate and apply these based on our biology. Our capacity to mediate environment and culture leads to creating beliefs and thereby, our values.

I've had the great fortune of implementing my 10 Life Values system into programs for men and fatherhood, women and motherhood; as well as youth and child-centered curriculum. To illustrate these values, let me present one man's journey that reveals how this system can be used every day to transform lives. Jay, a 33 year old, tells the story of his American Dream from a Black man's perspective utilizing the 10 Life Values system. Jay graduated from high school but remained uncertain about what he wanted to do in life. He yearned for the proverbial "more" in life, always searching for a better way. His dilemma was not having role models who were striving for excellence, who had a vision for greater ideals, nor a commitment to legacy building. Ten years ago being fed up with his stagnation, he called his friend, Bruce, who convinced him to move from New York to Los Angeles. Not only did Jay find opportunities there, but found refuge in the gangs of LA, which epitomized the lower socioeconomic status of success and power for young black men. He was destined for the wrong path until T. Rogers, the leader of the Black P Stone Bloods, pulled him aside and explained how this life was no place for him. He saw something unique in Jay that could positively impact the world, but he needed to return to the community and help other Black men rise above their current circumstances.

Armed with that advice, Jay set out to find and fulfill his purpose. Jay met Patrick Brown, one of the leaders in the community, who introduced him to the 10 Life Values program, with classes designed exclusively for men to motivate, inspire and transform them in three ways; 1) men ages 18-25 who are just starting out in life and need somewhere to begin, 2) men who are frustrated with their current results and want to fine-tune or even reinvent themselves, and 3) men who want to take their lives to the next level with the use of a proven system. These classes included organization, management, structure, accountability, and the use of technology. Upon graduation, Jay was given an accountability partner, Quentin, who would guide him in implementing the 10 Life Values, making it practical to his daily experiences and keeping him in progressive action. After working with Quentin for one year, Jay was invited to attend a 10 Life Values Conference to share his incredible journey to success in his own words.

With great confidence, Jay took the stage and shared his powerful story of his American Dream…

> "I grew up in New York, and always dreamed of being somebody important. I was average, but I knew that if I changed my environment I could go bigger and faster in life gaining success and riches. I struggled for a long time finding myself, and my purpose on this earth. I reveled in the gangsta lifestyle of LA but was fortunate to escape the tragedies of my fellow gang members who are now either dead or in prison. I languish in the thought that it could have been me. My mentor led me to the 10 Life Values, and there I learned what it truly meant to be a man.
>
> Even more impactful was learning that being a man meant learning to love and be loved, having courage, fellowshipping with other men, understanding struggle, overcoming adversity, coping with pain, taking a side and standing up for what's right. I now have a greater understanding of life and death, war, famine, diseases,

biology, culture, environment, honor, respect, and my spiritual journey. I also understand what it means to be good, masculine, brave, noble, adventurous, and learned how to address despair, resentment, envy, jealousy, lies, deceit, and injustice. My maturation process allowed me to gain greater insight into my choices, victories, wealth, women, sex, children, excellence, truth, having a belief and building a legacy. Furthermore, I needed to understand the issues specific to Black men and be smart enough to see the traps that lurked all around. These include low or no employment, incarceration, racial profiling, legal matters such as divorce, poor education, unhealthy relationships, lack of community support and identity; as well as black on black crime.

Once I understood that targeted black men lead to marginalized black men, because they have no other alternative or option but to destroy their community, I was better equipped to avoid these pitfalls. All of this insight showed me traps to avoid, particularly the trap of criminalization and underground existence characterized as lazy or giving up and resulting in a parasite existence, surviving off someone else. For instance, there was a war on drugs, but essentially it was a war on me, a black man. The U.S. economic system shut us out of the economy with ever-decreasing access to major industries; outsourcing jobs overseas, increasing the use of technology and automation. Additionally, nepotism further exacerbates the problem by carefully controlling and regulating jobs designed for a few handpicked blacks while the rest of us were abandoned in mass. So black men, like myself, are forced to turn to illegal activities as we are denied access to the legal economy. In reality, we have been maneuvered into these activities which are not good for the Black community nor America as a whole. Finding a way out demanded a strong system of values to reform my life.

Knowing this, Quentin, my 10 Life Values accountability partner, helped me process this devastating information about my reality, by coping with the stress and anxiety in my life through prayer and meditation. I started to grow spiritually and feel at peace even in the chaos of my environment. The 10 Life Values training opened my eyes to true unconditional love, forgiveness, patience and showed me the difference between being spiritual vs. religious. For the first time, someone cared enough to show me that my spiritual life was filled with negative energy which was holding me back from being successful. I learned that Spiritual Value is energy just like money is energy, and I wanted to understand how to get more of both of them. Quentin revealed how the 10 Life Values help me take real consistent action. I learned that when I can truly look at myself, look into myself with great examination and introspection, I have merely just begun to crack the rich code of my Spiritual Value.

Earlier this year, I felt pain and pressure in my chest. I hate going to the doctor, but I knew it was time. During my examination I went into cardiac arrest, the doctors rushed me to the hospital, and I was immediately taken into surgery. Then came the worse news I could hear at 33 years old - I had a heart attack with 99% obstruction in my left anterior descending artery, which causes the heart to stop quickly. I was very lucky to be alive…this was my wake-up call. It became very clear I had been eating myself to death. About two years ago, I was diagnosed with high cholesterol, then five months later my pressure was an alarming 170/100. Shortly after, my liver and pancreas started to fail, and just like the rest of my family, I got that dreaded disease, diabetes. All of this stress on my body affected organ after organ and uric acid built up in my blood, resulting in gout. I laid on my back looking up at the ceiling in the hospital room, but really looking up to God, and pleaded with Him to spare my life…I was too young to die.

The 10 Life Values helped me make a series of important changes:

- From not working out to exercising 10 minutes each morning to reduce stress, increase blood flow, strength and flexibility.
- From eating mostly meat and carbohydrates to juicing vegetables twice a week, eating more fruits, nuts, and grains.
- From drinking 4 cups of coffee and sodas to drinking 8 cups of water with minerals.
- From not using supplements to using an herbal solution called AGame, to increase my vitality, energy, strength, and libido, supporting proper blood flow to my organs.
- From not having control over my health to monitoring my body composition, weight, blood pressure, and sugar levels daily.

My progress is astounding, and I am cracking the rich code on my health well before my 35th birthday.

Family has always been an important part of my life. My biggest struggle was feeling anger towards my parents. For a long time, I hated my mother, in my opinion she was promiscuous and didn't value herself or me. I resented my father for making me feel like I had no value and leaving me to suffer while figuring out life without him. I was 8 years old. I waited all day and night for him to get me for the weekend. He never came…I didn't see him again until I became an adult. He died two years ago, I am coping with losing him, and dealing with my rage as I struggle to develop a family of my own. As long as

I stay transparent and remember the greatest parts of what it means to be a Black man, I can face social oppression and economic misfortune with optimism. Only then will I continue to crack the rich code on my Family Value.

I was always well-groomed and took pride in my appearance but was missing some essential wardrobe items as I expanded my circle of influence. For the first time in my life, I did an inventory on my clothes and accessories and learned how to keep my look relevant with quality items to reflect my value and orientation to life. My Appearance Value taught me that my behavior, attitudes, and how I showed up in the world were critical in navigating male spaces. Particularly as a Black man, my presence influenced my male rights, male survival, my rights of passage and fulfillment of my value. There has been a systematic dismantling of male spaces, but men are regaining the sanctity of spaces such as gyms, bars, barbershops, sports arenas, online and offline gaming, educational classes, to create community and protected environments for men to talk freely without judgment about issues, and participate in legacy teachings thorough fatherhood and mentorship. I am learning that my presence and participation, both verbally and through body language positions me for leadership, and if I continuously examine how I allow the world to see me then I will begin to crack the rich code of my Appearance Value.

As I continue to elevate myself it became clear that I needed to move to a safer community. My home has always been my castle even when I lived in the jungle of LA. It is now time to update my Dwelling Visionary Plan as I am moving from the bad side of town to the suburbs. I plan on adding exterior safety features, and internally create a peaceful environment in each room. I am doing well with making progress in cracking the rich code on my Dwelling Value.

One of the things I enjoyed about living in the city is the ease of getting around, but now living in the suburbs I will need to have a car to increase my Mobility Value. I will also have to meet the leadership in the new community, identify opportunities for civic engagement and leverage resources to gain upward mobility and not become isolated and immobilized. New adventures await me, and I will be purchasing a car that is dependable, reliable and holds its resale value. Quentin tells me a certified used Mercedes Benz might be the perfect fit for my vision. Making this purchase is a major investment for me, but I know how to work on cars, there is a service station not far from me, and I have a really good warranty so I believe I am truly cracking the rich code on my Mobility Value.

Standing before you today telling my story is a testament that if a barely passing high school graduate can change his life, you can too. Every day I am learning and increasing my Education Value. I am learning about spirituality, health, manhood, how to present myself to accomplish my pursuits, how to address and solve family matters, and I am learning about the importance of herbs for natural healing remedies and hair care. Now I have two all-natural hair products to help people in my community. I am crushing the rich code in my Education Value, and so excited about the next phase of my life.

Black men have to consider the dilemma of haphazardly participating in the illegal world or taking our chances in the legal world. In our communities we watch people navigate the waters of the underground life, but we also see those who struggle to thrive in the above-board life. Black men are plagued by socially engineered economic situations that deny legitimate means to employment and progress. People with education who hold advanced degrees and specialize in a particular field of expertise can either go to work for someone or go into business for themselves. The challenge is that industries are set up where Blacks don't have capital to start their own business or get a loan through conventional financing to expand their business. As a result, Black men who cannot generate income are pushed into a survival state. The Black male teen unemployment rate hovers at 90%, and in most major cities over 50% of adult Black males across the United States are unemployed. This is what I have to avoid at all costs. I struggled to advance professionally. However, Quentin worked with me on my Visionary Plan to help me get a more stable job. I applied for a job at the post office and got an interview. Now I work for the government with a great salary and benefits, but I can't stop here because I will never know when there will be layoffs and I feel more secure if my career was based on my own efforts. Nevertheless, I am cracking the rich code on Profession Value.

Some Black men struggle with leisure. Some of us either have too much time on our hands and play video games, go to clubs, attend social events, or engage in other non-income generating activities on a consistent basis. Other Black men work extremely hard holding down several jobs or putting in large amounts of overtime. The dilemma is that there was a generation of Black men who worked so hard they had little to no time to engage with their families or enjoy time to themselves. This resulted in the breakdown of the Black community. I am working towards excellence in every area of my life so I spend more time doing activities that rejuvenate me. I have a lot more to discover, but I am learning balance which will help me crack the rich code with my Leisure Value.

My most deflating experience of my connection with Quentin was when he asked me about the state of my Wealth Value. I really tried not to tell him how much I was struggling. I saw it as a question of my manhood. I wanted him to see me as a man of value doing well in life. I didn't want to feel the way my father made me feel…no value and would never be anybody of worth. Then one day Quentin turned to me and said, "Jay you are broke and struggling." I humbly replied, "Help me bro, I never want to struggle another day in my life". I had no savings, no investment portfolio, and very little retirement, but I had a lot of belief that I would make it big one day. He guided me as I developed my Wealth Visionary Plan and showed me how to take my herbal solutions and natural hair products hobby and turn it into a business while maintaining full-time employment. I got a tax ID for my company and started to build wealth. Once I understood that money is energy and I can exchange it for value I began to crack the rich code in my Wealth Value.

As the conference ends and I wrap up my talk, I realized what the 10 Life Values did for me in participating in our national ethos of the American Dream and creating a life of excellence as a Black man. I further realized the significance of that old African proverb, "If you want to go quickly, go alone. If you want to go far, go together." All this time I was under the impression that I could achieve success by myself, but nothing could have been further from the truth. I could not have achieved my personal American Dream without my father, my friends from the neighborhood, Bruce, T. Rogers, Patrick Brown, and Quentin. They truly were an important part of my journey towards achieving the value of my rich code."

***

To contact Dr. Holman:

phone: +1-951-515-5117

email: staff@fatherstime.com

website: www.fatherstime.com

LinkedIn: spencer-holman

Facebook: spencer.holman.77

Skype: spence767

YouTube: FathersTime

http://agameformen.com/

## Shirlene Reeves

Awarded the 'Exceptional Woman of Influence 2019' by the Women Economic Forum, Dr. Shirlene Reeves is a four-time award-winning author, media personality and motivational speaker who has journeyed from dumpster diving to diamonds. For 17 years she was the CEO of her own nationwide CA C Corporation, which she bootstrapped from zero to multi-millions with over 23,000 working under her. Dr. Shirlene specializes in teaching entrepreneurs, and coaches' strategies for building high income, heart-based communities that generate massive incomes. Today she travels the world, enjoys her Baja beach-front property and works with clients worldwide.

# Heart Based Selling for Financial Freedom

***By Dr. Shirlene Reeves***

It was a warm summer morning. I had just come in from a walk when Julia rang in for her appointment. While filling out my online form, Julia had shared her frustrations around her business income after two years of support from three coaches. I had chosen to meet with her to determine if she was having difficulty grasping and following through on the coaching she'd received or if there were missing pieces she hadn't yet learned and put into practice.

"Hi, Julia. How are you?" I asked with a big smile. "It's so great to meet you."

"Hi, Dr. Shirlene. Thank you for taking the time to meet with me. It's greatly appreciated."

"How can I help you, Julia?"

"As I mentioned on your form," she replied, "I'm frustrated. I feel like I'm not good enough to keep my business going. You would think with two years of coaching I'd be doing great, but I'm still not making enough money to quit my job. I can't figure out why."

"Well, let see what's missing. I agree that with three coaches it seems as though you should be doing quite well by now. What concerns you most?"

"My retirement account is practically gone, and I'm still working at my job to support my business. Every one of my coaches told me they'd be the last coach I'd ever need, but now all I've got is a bunch of debt. If things don't change, I'll be forced to give up my dream. Sarah referred me to you, and she's making boatloads of money, so I thought I'd ask you what to do."

"Let's make the most of our time together, Julia. Do you have programs that you're currently selling?"

"I have a bunch of programs, but that's part of the problem. I don't know which one to sell first. My last coach made me create a program every time something I said struck a chord with her. I've been told you can only sell one program at a time, so I'm really confused. How do I know which one to start with?"

"Some coaches aren't clear on how to integrate programs, so they work together," I responded calmly, noticing the edge in her voice. "Have you heard anything about how to integrate powerful programs?"

"No. No one mentioned that."

"With so many programs, there must be three you can integrate together."

"I don't even know what that means."

"I hear the frustration in your voice," I replied. "Let's slow down a bit and I'll clarify for you. You need three powerful integrated programs and one 'Easy Yes' program that acts like the front door."

"Oh, no, not another program. The last thing I need is another program."

"Please, let me give you an example based on my own programs. Maybe that will help. I have three powerful integrated programs and my $20 'Easy Yes' program. I do a webinar for $20 so potential clients have an hour to get to know, like, and trust me. People have no problem paying $20, and they get an hour of value similar to what I'm sharing with you. I teach the 'Easy Yes' course on Zoom to people all over the world. It's an excellent way to open a gateway to more sales, more clients, and more income."

"That's a great idea, and it doesn't seem like it would be difficult. I could easily invite people for only $20."

"It's easy once you know the formula. You also need to make sure you only invite people in your target market. Do you know who your target market is?"

"I think so, but I might need to focus more on that. I've been working with women between the ages of forty-five and sixty-five who have been laid-off."

"Have a lot of women been laid off at your company?"

"Yes. You wouldn't believe how many have been thrown out in the cold. I'm worried I might be next. That's part of why I'm so stressed."

"Do you think the women from your company might fit into your target market? Focusing in on a tightly defined target market makes a huge difference in your income. It's also an important ingredient in your sales process. Your goal, if I remember right, is to make more money so you can quit your job. Isn't that right?"

"Yes. My husband says I've already spent too much money and I need to start contributing to the household, but I don't see how that's possible. I like the idea of working with the women from my company because I already know them, but there may not be enough of them."

"How many is not enough?"

"I probably know about thirty of them pretty well."

"Thirty is a great start. Each person knows others they can refer to you."

"I see already that you know what you're doing," Julia said. "This is great information. How do you know all of this?"

"I've been coaching entrepreneurs for more than twenty-five years. I've had lots of time to experiment with sales and marketing. But it doesn't take long to learn how to speak a language your target market understands."

"What do you mean by that?" Julia was soaking up the information like a sponge.

"If you use words and phrases your clients don't understand, they won't hire you. One of my client's goals was to work with corporations and entrepreneurs. She was filling the room every time she held an event, but because she invited both entrepreneurs and corporate executives, she never got any business because they couldn't figure out what her message was. Once we pinpointed her message to speak only to corporate executives or entrepreneurs, she started getting $30,000 contracts. Now she's so busy we don't have time for coffee."

"I hear you, but I'm still not getting it. The message needs to be clearer."

"Funny girl! You just threw my own words back at me. Okay, let me clarify. When you take the time to interact with your target market, you become familiar with the words and phrases they use. Here's an example: When you are speaking to corporate executives, you refer to their team as employees. In the world of entrepreneurs, we identify them as virtual assistants, affiliates, and coaches.

"Companies call buyers customers. Entrepreneurs call them clients. You must speak a language your target perks up to and hears. That's how I call my clients to me from the stage. And guess what? I don't have to waste any time trying to chase my clients because they know what I do and where to find me."

"I can already see two glaring problems in my business," Julia said. "One is that I don't really know the language my clients use, and two, I haven't zeroed in on my target market properly. Why didn't the other coaches teach me this?" I could hear the annoyance in her voice.

"They may have told you, Julia. Sometimes we're so caught up in what we need to do next that we aren't zeroed in on the things we need to hear. We hear things when we're ready."

"Okay, I get that. I've been pretty overwhelmed. I feel like I'm being pulled every which way. As soon as I hear a great idea and think it's the right way to go, someone else gives me another great idea and I head off that way. I would be a lot less stressed if I felt confident about what I'm doing. I need to know step by step what to do. Then I can keep moving forward knowing I'm making progress by reaching each goal in the process. Tell me more about the programs please. I need to look through everything I've got and decide which ones work best. I might be able to combine some to make them more powerful."

"That's your next step, Julia. Your goal is to eliminate the feelings of being overwhelmed and zero in on the benefits your clients are looking for. After learning the words and phrases your target market uses, you'll need to ask them how you can support them. You want to know what they are looking for and then create programs to solve their problems and challenges. That is how you create programs that are easy to sell. One reason you are having challenges selling your programs is because you've got the process upside down. You've created programs, and now you're trying to find the people who need them. That's like looking for a needle in a haystack."

"Woohoo!" Julia exclaimed. "There really is a system to this. I love working with systems. I like checking off the boxes as I go along. Would you explain more about how to integrate my programs after the 'Easy Yes' webinar. I don't understand that process yet."

"Okay. When you do your 'Easy Yes' webinar, you will do what we call an up sell at the end. During the webinar, you need to seed your talk for your first program."

"You lost me again. Seeding? What does that mean?"

"Seeding means you structure your talk, so it makes sense to move into your subsequent programs. In other words, I might say something like:

"One of the most important things you can do after deciding on your target market and putting your three programs together is to learn how to sell them. What if you could sell your programs without rejection? That would be awesome, wouldn't it?

"That statement seeds the importance of taking the sales course so you can learn how to sell without rejection."

"Got it. So, I have to give hints about my next program so people will get to know what's in it before I tell them about it at the end of the 'Easy Yes'."

Julia was excited that she was beginning to understand the process and what she needed to improve her own system.

"How much should my first program be?" she asked.

"Wow," I replied. "You are asking an eight-hour class of questions. Thanks for keeping me on track. The next program should be priced anywhere from $497 to $1,497. Any higher and your clients will experience sticker shock. When their eyes look like saucers and they begin to back away, you are charging too much for the time it's taken to know, like, and trust you. How much is your first program?"

"All of my programs are $197. Would you tell me more about how to integrate my programs?"

"The $197 price point works, but it could be higher if you make your first program meatier. Maybe you have two or three programs you could put together for $497. My other two courses integrate with the Heart-Based Sales course. I have a six-month Business Mastery course centered around the creation of three integrated programs, and a four-month video media course. This course is designed specifically for clients desiring to create video messaging while interviewing on podcasts, web TV, and webinars. They become guest experts in their specialized areas of expertise and make money all over the world. While gaining knowledge in these courses, my students soon realize the importance of taking the sales course to become knowledgeable in seeding their programs during their interview messaging."

"Dr. Shirlene, what do I do about sales? I hate feeling pushy, and I'm always afraid to ask for the money. Even when I have the right programs, I know I won't know how to sell them. Every attempt I've made in the past resulted in a no. It makes me want to run and hide. You just mentioned that you teach how to sell without getting rejected."

"Maybe you should consider taking my course. Making sales seems to be one of the most difficult challenges business owners experience. I have some theories about that. Would you like to hear them?"

"Absolutely. I hate sales, so anything you can tell me would make a difference—I hope."

"Most small business owners fear rejection more than any part of the sales process. It hurts our feelings when our friends and family turn us down or hide out in an attempt to avoid eye contact for fear of being pressured into a sale.

"Clients come to me frequently saying, 'I was asked to coffee the other day by a new friend. I was excited that this person wanted to get to know me, but then I found out all he wanted was to sell to me. It wasn't about becoming friends at all, and now I'll never work with that person. I couldn't get out of there fast enough.' Okay, I embellished that a bit, but you get the idea.

"There's an art to building relationships into sales. If you do it correctly, your clients will call you to ask for your support instead of you chasing and pressuring them into a sale. Hammering on people to buy from you is a sure way to ruin friendships and wind up lonely, broke, and out of business.

"Building relationships before sales will change the dynamics of your friendships, sales, and referral relationships. When you get to know people with love in your heart and show a genuine interest, you will foster great referral connections. You can easily overcome rejection by building meaningful relationships prior to mentioning what you do in business. Ask questions, listen to the answers, and do what you can to avoid monopolizing the conversation."

"I love making new friends," Julia replied, "but the fear of rejection is always there. I don't even know why I'm so afraid, or where the fear came from."

"I have a theory for why we dislike sales and fear rejection. Would you like to hear it?"

"Please."

"We're told 'No' throughout our formative years. No, don't take your brother's toys. No, you aren't swimming today. No candy today. No, no, no. That's a time of exploration in our lives, but we're challenged by the many nos that conflict with our natural curiosity.

"Being sent to our room to think about what we've done wrong creates a sense of rejection. Behaviors punished with alienation instill a belief that we're bad children. We are managed while being taught to agree and behave as expected by the social norm."

"I never thought about it that way," said Julia. "I was sent to my room a lot. I felt very alone and rejected thinking I was a bad girl. That must be why I feel like I'm not good enough."

"That's exactly what happens. As adults, we become people pleasers, believing we'll never be liked if we don't agree or do as others wish. We resist being told no, fear being rejected, and avoid the sales process.

"I constantly hear people selling without realizing it. They recommend places to eat, movies, and hairstylists. So why is it difficult to recommend your programs? It's the fear of no. But as I mentioned before, you can compel your clients to call you by building heart-based relationships while showing people you care."

"No one ever taught me how to compel people to want my programs," Julia chimed in with an exuberant aha.

"Start building relationships with potential clients before you launch into your sales pitch. In my book *Selling Through Your Heart*, I wrote about the Three Step Sales Waltz™. It's the technique I've used for more than twenty-five years to build relationships that convert into sales. Many entrepreneurs ask me how I make so many sales. That's why I decided to lay out my system step by step. In 2019, my book won three prestigious awards."

"If I understand you correctly, you're saying I should focus on making new friends instead of selling? Doesn't that waste a lot of time?"

"The sales process is not about selling your programs. It's about connecting with others using your heart-based listening skills. You can help everyone you meet, knowing they are either a sale for you or a referral for your affiliate team."

"Affiliate team? Where do I find them?"

"If you don't have an affiliate team, you are leaving a lot of money on the table. An affiliate team is a group of business owners you've taken the time to interact with, learn in depth what they do, and feel confident referring. If you listen carefully to those you meet, you'll be able to refer them to a member of your team and make an affiliate fee. Then your time is never wasted.

"All some people do is refer people and earn referral fees. They don't bother creating programs of their own because they are much better at connecting the people who fit others' needs. They simply make a lot of friends and live on referral fees. I call it partying for profit. All you need to do is attend events and put people together. But don't forget to negotiate your referral fees first."

"That would be fun. I'm going to start building my team right away."

"I have one last thought for you, and then I need to meet with my next client."

"Okay."

"Always keep in mind that you can do whatever you imagine. When you imagine it and write it down, your mind begins working toward your dream. Suddenly, synchronicities pop up, people open new doors, and with persistence and focus, your dreams begin to come true. If you are passionate about your sales goals, while focusing on what you imagine, you will surely be able to quit your job."

"How do I start working with you?"

"Get your free sales starter kit at https://heartbasedselling.com. I look forward to seeing you in my next class."

Within nine months after this conversation, Julia succeeded in quitting her job, contributing to the household expenses, and reaching $125,000 in sales.

"Congratulations, Julia. I'm proud of you," I told her.

"Thanks so much, Dr. Shirlene," she replied. "With your system, it was easy."

***

To contact Shirlene:

Get Dr. Shirlene's book Selling Through Your Heart: http://bit.ly/SellingThroughYourHeart

Book Dr. Shirlene to Speak: https://bookshirlene.com

Take the Heart-Based Selling Quiz: http://bit.ly/HeartBasedSalesQuiz

# Amy Oppedisano

Amy Oppedisano is a co-founder of the first publicly traded cannabis company in the U.S. After her husband fractured a vertebra in his neck in a surfing accident, doctors prescribed opioids to ease the pain. He couldn't stand the feeling of the pills and the couple worried about the dangers of addiction. They turned to cannabis to relieve the pain, a decision that ultimately altered the course of their lives. This life-altering injury was the catalyst for the couple to leave their careers in 2010 and launch Terra Tech Corp.

As a true believer in cannabis, Amy has always pursued a path helping other Americans to have the same choice available to them when it came to pain relief. Before she was on the ground floor of the legal cannabis revolution, Amy made her career in interior design with an emphasis on residential construction management. As a real estate entrepreneur Amy has successfully flipped over $8 million in residential real estate. Her work has been published by several major blogs and has been featured in Architectural Digest Germany. Amy served on the Board of Directors for Terra Tech Corp from 2012-2017 and is one of the first female founders of a publicly traded cannabis company. In 2019 Amy used her position in the marketing department at Terra Tech to focus on promotions that encouraged social responsibility while giving back to the community, including organizing the launch of Mission Green. Mission Green is a non-profit organization that seeks to provide relief for those incarcerated for nonviolent cannabis offenses.

## Redefining the Idea of Wealth

***By Amy Oppedisano***

In order to become wealthy, you must first become rich. At first glance this statement may seem silly and entirely unhelpful. If you purchased this book, it is my assumption you are here to learn to make more money. The most valuable lesson on my own quest to become wealthy over the last ten years has been to redefine the concepts of richness and wealth. I truly believe this mentality is the fundamental building block to success. Over the course of my chapter, I will walk you through some of my greatest challenges and how they shifted my perspective to understand why we crave these achievements and ultimately, how to obtain them. I believe if you can manage to do this for yourself, you too will be successful beyond your wildest dreams.

At the age of twenty-eight I co-founded the first plant-touching publicly traded cannabis company in the United States. After the collapse of the housing market in 2008 I found myself out of work and married to a man (also my co-founder, Derek Peterson) with a very serious injury whose medical care I was overseeing. He had fractured a vertebra in his neck in a surfing accident which left him unable to work for months as he suffered through chronic debilitating pain. We went to every orthopedist we could find, and yet traditional medicine had very few options for us. There were risky surgeries that could only promise a 30% chance of improving the pain. The only other alternative was to delay surgery and live on opiates for the foreseeable future. I find myself shocked to this day that in an innovative country like ours, we still battle stigma surrounding cannabis while opiates remain the only option for many sufferers of chronic pain. We knew this could not be the only answer and his devastating injury led us to discover the true medicinal value of cannabis. I am embarrassed to admit that prior to this experience I had assumed California's legalization of medical cannabis was simply a ruse for stoners to get high. I could not have been more wrong and am grateful that as Californians we had the freedom to treat his pain with cannabis. I am now extremely proud to say that medicinal cannabis has kept my husband opiate-free for 13 years and counting.

As idealistic young entrepreneurs fueled with our newfound passion for medical cannabis, we jumped headfirst into the industry. I had been an interior designer with a knack for running small businesses and managing large scale construction projects. My husband had worked in finance and knew the ins and outs of raising capital and running public companies. We knew we had something to offer the industry, which at that time was a far cry from something that mainstream America would easily embrace without skepticism and fear. By sharing our story, we could educate and help other Americans who were suffering like Derek. With our efforts concentrated on advancing national legalization while simultaneously building our business, we were able to fulfill our personal goal of broadening others' access to this plant that had performed a miracle for us.

All startups have their challenges, but cannabis is a federally illegal Schedule 1 narcotic according to the US Government, and I grossly underestimated how challenging this would be and in hindsight, that is a good thing! Any normal human being assumes a risk like this with some trepidation; however, I have seen fear easily outpaced by the passion to succeed especially when your pursuit is in service to something bigger than yourself. The first time I visited a dispensary to vend cannabis, we were robbed at gunpoint by eight men who had set up a fake shop in order to steal from vendors. Afterwards we called the local police, and were responded to nonchalantly with a simple "what did you expect"? To make matters worse, the officer on the other end of the line laughed and subsequently hung up on me.

At the time I had no idea that was only the beginning of the challenges we would face. Cannabis was all over the news in those days and we quickly found out it was nowhere near as 'legal' as the mainstream media had led us to believe. This was a world where everyone had been operating in the underground for decades and it was as lawless as the Wild West. There are some great people in the industry who have the best of intentions, but we did not experience too many of those people in our early days in cannabis. We were stolen from and taken advantage of in ways that I never could have imagined. Most days it seemed like anything that was not nailed down was taken by anyone from bad business partners, to vendors and customers, even some of our own employees whose bank fraud and hacking skills were far more impressive than their work ethics. This is where I learned of the term "friendly-fraud", which means certain financial transaction platforms offer no protections if the person who stole from you is someone you know. I cannot say that I kept my cool through any of these challenges in the early days, and any long-term entrepreneur knows they are not unique to our business and they will always exist. What matters is how you learn to navigate them, most importantly not allowing them to cause permanent emotional damage or resentment within yourself.

While I was very naïve to this world I had willingly stepped into, I was uniquely suited to survive it. At the beginning of seventh grade I began getting severely bullied at school. In those days teachers and parents turned a blind eye to it and I was told to simply ignore it. I went through all of junior high without a single friend at school and the feelings of insecurity from that experience followed me for many years after. To this day I can undeniably attribute this challenging part of my life to be one of the most valuable gifts I was ever given. I went through my most formative years learning to how build the mental fortitude to endure hard situations for long stretches of time. It also made me fiercely independent and able to ignore the opinions of others, instead trusting in myself because I had gotten myself through tough times on my own before. If you can train your mind to endure challenges as if the process is like training for a marathon as opposed to a sprint, you too can achieve this measure of fortitude. It is helpful to adopt an ability to look at everything you go through from a lens of gratitude. This is not always easy to do and sometimes that perspective does not come until months, even years later. A great businessperson will always be able to see the lesson in every situation and use it as a tool to move forward. If you can build an internal strength from each and every experience, positive or negative, you will wake up one day and realize you are a total badass. In order to retain this perspective, I like to meditate on some of nature's most stunning creations, all of which are the result of years of intense grit or pressure.

It took me a long time to wake up to this insight, so I am hoping that by sharing my experience it will shorten your learning curve. The word "rich" has a definition so incredibly broad that it seems created intentionally to define my concept of wealth. This is a word that can be used to describe everything from the beautiful colors of a sunset to the depth of flavor in the best meal you have ever eaten. If we are setting out to become rich, why would we only want material wealth? If your life can be rich in everything you do, then you are truly living. When I finally woke up to that understanding, the hurt I was carrying around from these challenging times began to dissolve into a knowledge that these moments made me who I am. In Buddhist teachings these are called Kensho moments. Kensho is the concept of "growth through pain". It is thought to be our soul's wake up call to our human selves, a tough self-love of sorts. I have now realized that was exactly what I had needed at that point in time to achieve the wealth I wanted. The difference being, my definition of wealth had now shifted, and I would not have arrived here without my Kensho moments.

I now know that the true value of my life lies within me and that I am truly wealthy because I have created something that no one can take from me. To me this means an inner richness that can be applied to every facet of life in a positive or productive manner. If you are able to do this, you will give yourself a life more fulfilling than you ever could have imagined and if that isn't wealth, I don't know what is. Because of what I have gained through taking a risk on my business, I can now live my life with a level of confidence and strength that you cannot learn from a book, a class or another person. No matter where I go or what I attempt to accomplish, I know that I have earned the skillsets necessary to be successful in that endeavor. I unintentionally put myself through a decade worth of tests that I never even knew I needed.

This mental fortitude that I had earned through repeated trials of endurance, has been my greatest asset in being able to stay in such a challenging industry for ten years. If your inner richness is made up of earned confidence, as opposed to ego driven behaviors that are rooted in insecurities, you will be able to lead your business in a way that remains true to your own vision without being swayed by the opinions of others. This is especially difficult when you are doing something in the public eye where you open yourself up to the opinion of everyone who has a Wi-Fi connection. If you are vulnerable to being affected by this, you will easily get sucked out of your workflow into unproductive negative emotions that can take over and pull you off course. In order to remain steadfast, you must always remind yourself that you are the only one with a full 360-degree view of your business. You must make decisions constantly using information that only you have. The observers are simply observing. Your Kensho moments will not profoundly impact the life of the observer, they must create those for themselves. If you want richness for your life you must get in the arena and participate, while not worrying about the opinions of those who only bought a ticket to watch.

The advent of social media has amplified the voice of these observers, as well as created an environment that overfeeds the ego and bombards us with a "get rich quick" cultural mentality. Social media has also brought us inspiration, innovation and motivation from all sorts of people who now have a free platform for creating their own greatness. The playing field of business is very similar. If you enter into your business with the proper mentality you can generate an inspired and fulfilled life no matter how it pans out, but maintaining the proper perspective is the key. Kylie Jenner is a billionaire at 22 years old, and many people succumb to the pressure of thinking they are a failure if they cannot keep up with that unrealistic pace. The fundamental flaw with the "get rich quick" mentality is that it relies upon luck and unfortunately luck is random. No one in their right mind should rely solely on luck to create their fortunes and no one should ever beat themselves up internally because luck did not pan out. If you can approach your business from the mentality that no matter what happens you will get rich, because you have properly defined richness and are honing the skillsets necessary to earn it, then you have nothing to lose! That being said, the greatest failure I can imagine is achieving worldly success without simultaneously achieving internal peace and happiness. The unhappy wealthy person is a societal cliché portrayed in art, poetry and theater for thousands of years. Marie Antoinette spent her days pretending to be a peasant, which I imagine was born out of the fantasy that a simpler life would provide her with something she did not have through the mechanism of material wealth - happiness. If the path to financial success does not simultaneously provide internal happiness and self-satisfaction, then you have built a house of cards. Money can vanish for a wide variety of reasons and if that was the only thing keeping you happy, your inner peace will vanish with it. If you have built a solid foundation of internal richness, you will never be broke, no matter what your bank account says that day.

While we have faced a multitude of challenges over the years, filing for bankruptcy was one of the most impactful. This experience felt like utter failure at the time, yet I am now able to appreciate it wholeheartedly for the lessons I learned in the process. In 2008 my husband was working for a large national bank, one of those whose signage is now occupying a landfill somewhere. When the economy collapsed, we personally suffered a complete economic wipeout, watching helplessly as our nest egg evaporated and our income dried up. We struggled to recuperate financially over the following years while supporting our business, but eventually the substantial losses had taken their toll and we had no other choice but to file for bankruptcy while I was a few months pregnant with my second child. The most humbling experience of my life was taking my one year old with me to stock up on paper products, canned foods and other non-perishables with our few remaining dollars so that we could survive until we got back on our feet. I walked out of the store with my shopping cart and when I stepped away to place my son in his car seat, the cart took off rolling down the parking lot crashing into a curb and spilling everything onto the ground. I instantly felt that the risk I had taken in starting this company had completely backfired on me. I had felt so defeated in that moment I just stood there and cried. Two men in business suits rushed to help me clean it all up, loading my car for me while I just watched in tears. I will never forget this moment as long as I live because I was humbled in a way that I never could have learned without going through it.

These kinds of experiences can turn conventional wisdom into true knowledge that moves you to the core of your being. Because I went to what felt like the bottom and later climbed back out, I have built for myself a measure of confidence and strength that no matter what happens I have the ability to solve it and come out better on the other side. The human ego cannot provide this for you. It is designed to keep you physically safe by narrating an internal warning system that if left unchecked can extrapolate everyday nuisances or insecurities into "fight or flight" situations. This is where taking that leap and going through everything your business puts on your plate helps to defeat ego-based insecurities while turning you into a solid rock of confidence. Things are only scary when they are entirely unknown. Once you experience them and come out the other side, the fear is gone, and the annoying voice of the ego is quieted. This brings about inner peace. Allowing your mind to embrace these experiences from a place of gratitude, no matter how bad it feels at the time, will provide you with the richness you are craving. From that point on you will carry this richness with you like an internal cheat sheet for creating your desired material wealth. Without possessing the tools to create that wealth, you would always live in fear of losing something you could never get back. For this reason, I would never actually want to become successful as a matter of luck!

The concepts of money and wealth have been created by humanity and you are a human – you have the option to redefine what these constructs mean to you! Once you have experienced the path to earning true wealth you will likely find that your priorities change. You have an internal confidence that doesn't drive you to purchase the expensive watch or fancy sports car out of insecurity. If you want those things it is entirely okay, however when the ethos behind obtaining them is based on the pride you feel by truly earning them, you will find them far more satisfying. I believe that the key to Cracking the Rich Code is to first crack yourself wide open. Examine everything you see, both past and present, from a place of gratitude, humility and a desire to become a better person and you will possess the keys to unlocking success simply by being exactly who you already are. If you have a dream or an idea, all you need to do is go for it. Accept whatever happens next as extremely valuable and keep going for it every day after that. In doing so you will turn yourself into your own greatest asset. You will not regret building internal strength, skillsets and values that absolutely no one can take away from you.

Thank you from the bottom of my heart for reading these words, I hope they are helpful to you and I wish you the best in all your future endeavors!

***

To contact Amy:
Instagram: @amy_oppedisano
Linked In: Amy Oppedisano

# Evan Sanchez

Evan Sanchez is the CEO of Springboard Consulting, a management consulting firm based out of Flower Mound, Texas. His "Intuitive Flow" coaching psychology has been implemented in Leadership and sales skill development programs, corporate wellness, and executive coaching producing performance revenue increases of 47% on average. This high-performance mindset is currently outlined in his book- Sell like a Champ that focuses on building the top mindsets, toolsets, and skillsets for peak performance in sales.

As a board advisor and strategic growth partner of ThinkX, Evan works to implement the ground-breaking nuero-science of performance drivers as a next level coaching tool and human capital strategy to build a Culture of A players who perform at high levels and Think Like Champs!

With more than 25 years as an entrepreneur, sales professional, personal trainer, coach and as a former member of semi-professional Albuquerque Gunners soccer team, Sanchez knows all about setting goals and the champion mindset necessary to achieve new levels of success.

In addition to a bachelor's degree with special study in sports psychology from Texas Tech and the University of North Texas, he's been the owner or co-owner of three businesses, director of sales and marketing and senior consultant with global consulting firm Kepner-Tregoe, sales manager at LandAmerica American Title, and a sales director at The Dallas Business Journal.

Evan lives with his wife and three children.

## Why "A-Players" Win at Business:

## Cracking the code of human behavior and performance

***By Evan Sanchez***

Every successful business grows at scale when it has top performers in key positions, delivering consistently outstanding work. Studies show that most people who perform in the top 10% of a company would do well almost anywhere and that they work fewer hours than those in the bottom 20%. Further studies show that there are key behaviors and thinking capabilities that make some people a better fit than others in different positions. The "performance dilemma" could have disastrous results to the bottom line, if left unattended. The ability to separate winners from losers and optimize your workforce is critical.

What are the characteristics of these high performers and what can you do to boost your own performance to the top 10% level? What can you do to Think Like A Champ? What can you do to address the performance optimization in your entire team or organization?

The top 10% have a "play to win" mentality. They believe they cannot fail. They believe that they can only learn and grow as they compete with themselves. They are driven not by a fear and scarcity mindset, but a positive belief that it is impossible for them to lose and in every struggle, there is a lesson in success to apply that builds strength to persevere.

Do such people even exist? You may be one of them, but chances are that the previous paragraph caused you to pause and even feel anxious. The good news is that it is possible to figure out your core thinking – which drives emotion, and how you feel determines how you show up, and take action. The innate desire for success can cause frustration if your own thinking is preventing you from achieving it.

It starts with you - The Essential Power of Self Belief

As a business leader the ability to develop self-confidence – that of a top 10% performer – is a key ingredient. It is built from self-belief.

If you don't believe in yourself, it could even be perceived instead as a lack of belief in your product or service. When you lack self-belief, it fuels a downward spiral of actions – because thinking drives your emotion and soon your ability to influence and persuade others dwindles. In turn, the lack of success negatively affects your belief in what you are selling, creating a cycle of negativity and doubt that makes it harder and harder to succeed.

It is easy to start blaming external factors for lack of success, and granted, in some cases they may well be at play. However, you are the central force in your own life. No matter what happens around you, you do have control over your response to the world and all it's circumstances. Central to your power of taking ownership for your own success, is healthy thinking and a mindset of growth and resilience. We call this a Champion Mindset – most common to the top 10% of those who win at business. Before you can embrace that mindset however, it's necessary to know how to recognize and overcome the barriers that hold you back.

Recognizing Barrier (aka "Stinking") Thinking

When negative beliefs and thoughts take hold, there is a domino effect of negativity for you, others around you, and your company culture. Often, we forget that our perceptions are not necessarily reflective of reality. Indeed, our thoughts and beliefs are built through a complicated pattern of neural pathways, created from life experiences. Those pathways create the internal narrative, the self-talk, that influences our behaviors. Barrier thinking is the root cause of low performance.

When your thinking is negative, or causes barriers to healthy action, others perceive you in that light. Their perceptions about you become negative and influence their behaviors toward you – which only serves to "confirm" your negative perceptions about yourself. This barrier thinking "spiral" can be debilitating to you, and your team.

When stinking thinking goes unchecked, even high performing people can become toxic, eroding their own confidence and success over time, and negatively influencing others around them. Beyond stellar smarts, ability, strengths and a "play to win" mentality, top performers can persevere and thrive in the face of the same market and environmental challenges that others find insurmountable. The key? They recognize moments of "stinking thinking" and can reframe those thoughts in a healthy, outcome-oriented way. To re-frame something internal, takes instant recognition.

The chart below includes some of the most common examples of stinking thinking, along with the healthy/reality focused approach that a top 10% performer would take in the same situation.

| | |
|---|---|
| I've never done it before. | It's an opportunity to learn something new. |
| It's too complicated. | I'll tackle it from a different angle and break it into simpler steps. |
| I don't have the resources. | I do know where to find what I need, and I can work with what I have. |
| I'm too lazy to get this done. | I am procrastinating out of fear. I will prioritize the time to just start with the first step. |
| There's no way it will work. | I will look for ways to succeed at it. |
| It's too radical a change. | I'm willing to take a step toward this new idea. |
| No one bothers to communicate with me. | I will communicate with others in a positive way. |
| I'm not going to get any better at this. | I'm learning and will get better in time. |
| My way is the better way. | I will be open to others' ideas and suggestions – maybe I can learn from them. |
| People won't like me if I do that. | Even if people disagree with my idea, they still like or accept me. |

## Shifting Thinking & Behavior Toward Success – The Challenge

The solution appears relatively simple - if we can learn to identify our stinking thinking and the associated triggers, we can use those moments to re-frame our narrative to a positive, solution-oriented focus. However, that approach merely addresses the surface issues, rather than delving into the thinking patterns that are the root cause of stinking thinking and self-sabotage.

Our root source thinking patterns are often sub-conscious, making it difficult to correct and develop real independence and belief in self in a sustainable way. How can we move to not having the barrier thought to begin with? Re-framing, while helpful, in the moment, can become exhausting and when we are under any kind of stress or pressure, we default to what's most familiar – the stinking thinking.

"You can't solve problems using the same type of thinking we used when we created them."– Albert Einstein

Creating realistic perceptions and performance-enhancing thinking patterns can re-ignite confidence, increase drive, develop mental toughness, and build resilience.

If you have implemented programs for yourself or others to improve performance, you know that it's possible to train, practice and coach to improve skills that enhance performance, at least in the short term. We can learn about the market, competition, and to be creative problem solvers and expert advisors. All these things can build self-confidence in a person and you may even see temporary positive results, but until you also develop the underlying thinking patterns, you may see a regression in the people trained, and you may miss the opportunity for more lasting behavior change.

Therein lies the apparent challenge of not being able to measure or re-orient what appears to be internal and immeasurable. It isn't easy cracking the code of what makes someone or keeps someone performing at an A, B or C level.

The key to success rests on an individual's performance thinking. Performance thinking links directly to the intangible qualities we often struggle to describe – we sometimes refer to it as the "IT" factor or "Self-Starters" - will, heart, drive, versatility, agility and more. People either have it, or they don't. It's hard to measure, and sometimes impossible to predict.

What does this mean for the growing organization?

At the front end of your human capital strategy, this presents challenges in hiring top talent. It requires the courage to let go of hiring practices that were based on gut feelings and even corporate traditions, rather than measurable performance data. Even stringent implementation of behavioral assessments, fact and results-based interviewing and rigorous pre-hire testing have failed to give company leaders high rates of success in hiring the best performers more than 90% of the time.

Another challenge for organizations is creating a common performance language for the culture and driving employee engagement around the performance improvement process, while also linking those to capabilities, developmental paths, and measurable results. Due to the soft skill nature of many of these capabilities, it is very difficult to show ROI and quantitative data. You may know success when you see it, but that doesn't mean you can replicate it.

The solution - Performance Thinking Neuroscience & Strategies

Discoveries in neuroscience have made the visibility and measurement of performance thinking possible. This type of data can identify the specific thinking patterns that directly impact performance, in any position, and have been validated and field tested for two decades. These discoveries have led to defined Performance Drivers™ (groups of neural pathways proven to drive certain thinking and resultant outward behavior) that are used to predict performance in a quantitative and measurable way. These measurements also give us tools to quantify performance capacity and effectively hire, develop, and audit talent to the level of the current "A players" or top 10% of performers at the organizational or functional level.

Objectivity of data measurement and scientifically proven predictability takes the guesswork out of your hiring. It measures everyone equally, against the desired outcomes for any position. It removes any unconscious bias in decision-makers during hiring, and positively impacts diversity and inclusion. When measured against a set of Performance Drivers, there is no subjective date to add "noise" to the hiring considerations. The measurement of a thinking algorithm in the brain will also give you predictable patterns of stress (aka stinking thinking) that may exist and often don't surface until an individual has been working for you for several months. This stress can lead to dis-ease and health issues in the future that can also seriously impact the bottom line.

How do you start using performance thinking neuroscience strategies?

Each employee starts with a personal benchmark of score ranges in each of these Performance Drivers. By analyzing the profiles of the top 10% of performers in each role, the data will point to conclusions about what these individuals have in common that makes them successful in the organization.

From there, it's possible to extrapolate what specific types of performance coaching would help the other 90% better align their performance thinking with that of the top 10%.

By identifying and defining the underlying characteristics that make individuals successful in a specific role, within a specific organization, individual performance can be framed in terms of developing adaptability, versatility, ability to manage stress, and drive. Rather than repeatedly sending a group through skills training, everyone receives feedback and clinically validated coaching to develop the tools to trade up underlying barrier (stinking) thinking patterns holding them back from success. Individuals will develop thinking patterns that lead to real independence, ambition, confidence and success. They develop the will and ability to win.

Through a combination of individual and team data, managers can benchmark and measure performance improvements, identify leaders and provide employees with personalized, actionable feedback that they can relate to their day-to-day activities. In other words, a much larger part of the core will become A Players.

Proven Results = Sustainable success

Empirical data exists from a successful implementation of this science for two decades, in multiple companies, across diverse industries. People collectively can make or break your business – starting with you. Success doesn't happen through force, nor through luck. Success happens when you crack the code of human sciences that for the past century has remained a misnomer – a soft skill, immeasurable, fuzzy, "touchy feely" – to name a few words used to describe human behavior.

It would be important to address the existence of powerful and worthy tools that help identify behavior – from personality, to problem solving methods, to styles, strengths, motivators, team values, etc. These tools are valuable for building and optimizing work teams, from leadership to the front lines. What has been missing is knowing the "why" behind behavior. Just know what "it" is, has not helped solve the challenges that "it" may pose, in the context of performance and contribution to the company goals.

Bottom line – it's all about thinking

Getting to results is the driving force behind most entrepreneurs and business leadership, as it should be. Knowing the levers that help or hinder performance that contributes to those results requires taking a step back. Getting to the indicators and knowing how to re-frame thinking means taking yet another step back.

It could look a bit like this:

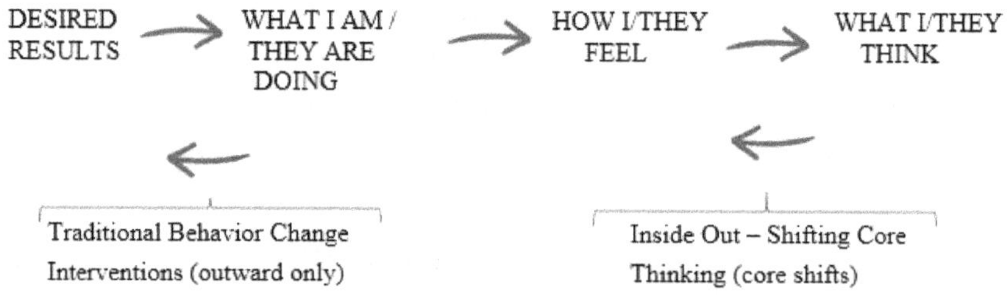


Revolutionizing the human development and human capital process provides leaders with the data, the tools, and the proven methodology design the desired Culture; to build A-teams consistently, to drive exponential growth in themselves, their teams, and their entire enterprise.

Springboard Consulting focuses on "Elevating Thinking to Elevate Business" performance. Our partnership with 10Rule allows us to offer the ground-breaking neuro-science and SaaS based behavioral tools to identify and coach to the performance drivers that lead to success and replace those that can hold you or your team from thinking like a champ. You can learn to "Think Like a Champ" and Crack the Rich Code with an individual assessment and strategy session geared to springboard your leadership and organizational performance. When we remove known and unknown barriers to success, business performance will Springboard to new heights. If you would like to learn the What, Why and How to build a team of A players give us a shout. We look forward to helping you Be A Champ!

***

To contact Evan:

Evan Sanchez

CEO, Springboard Consulting

Author and Speaker

Phone: 972-977-2140

Evan@SellLikeAChamp.com

www.Springboard.Consulting

Chris McSwain

CEO & Co-Founder

10rule, Inc.

Phone: 269.281.1120

Chris.mcswain@10rule.com

www.10Rule.com

## Dr. Thomas S. Heemstra

Dr. Thomas S. Heemstra has authored several published works:

STARQuest Character Education and Leadership Development Curriculum

Anthrax: A Deadly Shot in the Dark: Unmasking the Truth Behind a Hazardous Vaccine

The Change, Volume 7: The Words and the *Bees* of Bold Transformational Change!

Cracking the Rich Code Vol #2, Chapter 7. "Wealth of Connections Conquer Circumstances, Chaos, and Corruption."

Upcoming books: The 7 Rights to … (Ethics) ~ I-25 Innovation Drive, the Creator's Road ~

Transformational Leadership Development: … the Story

Tom is a former F-16 Fighter Squadron Commander with 15 combat missions in Iraq, a graduate of the U.S. Air Force Academy with a Doctorate degree in Strategic Leadership from Regent University. Tom is Founder of MACH 5 Leadership Solutions, an executive coaching and organizational leadership consulting business. He is a former Outstanding Adjunct Professor in Servant Leadership at the College of Mt. St. Joseph in Cincinnati and is a Senior Associate for GiANT Worldwide.

He is Founder of *Creator's University*, a creative thinktank to help businesses with innovation, problem solving, and creativity; and help teen students achieve their creative dreams. He was also Founder of the *The Sanctuary*, a not-for-profit retreat center designed for wounded leaders and injured soldiers returning home, and burnt-out pastors and missionaries. Tom is an International Airline Captain with over 20,000 flying hours. He lives near Knoxville Tennessee on gorgeous Norris Lake with his wife, Alise. And plays Pickleball at every opportunity!

# Cracking the "Rich" Code

## Like Everest, But a Better Mountain

***Dr. Thomas S. Heemstra***

"Multiple Climbers Dead!"

Mt. Everest at 29,000 feet is topping today's headlines. What went wrong for these climbers?

"Startling!" Driver John shrieked to CEO-selectee, Mr. Gropper during their daily traffic jaunt. "Just to get to the top, why?"

Good question Gropper thought beginning his journey. Why always climbing, only to risk it all?

"How about you, Mr. Gropper: Got your ladder leaning on the right wall?!" quipped Driver John, with his allegorical challenge.

Penetrating, unnerving; afraid of both: to die, or to fail, Hass could only hand-signal, "Touché!"

*Bidoop...bidoop*, the sound of windshield wipers sweeping snow off the limo glass lulling Mr. Gropper's thoughts into la-la-land. Reluctantly Hass surrendered conscious control.

*Bidoop and Swoosh.* Helicopter blades strained for a high-altitude touchdown at Everest Base Camp, landing skids yearning for safe and solid ground. Back at home-office everyone assumed Everest a worthy destiny for a future CEO. Was he just complying with their expectations, his own; or both?

Industry-record performance put Hass here at Base Camp, 17,500' above sea level where the real ascent-journey begins. With amazingly minimal costs on paper, he left behind littered trails of countless, crumbling relationships. And what was left, was not right.

Hass thought on his ladder to success, the brokenness, wounds, scars, and skeletons from relationships past came with the territory. Buried in frozen, nearly forgotten memories; his acute smell for 'blood-in-the-water' fear, as an executive shark effectively terrorized the competition, intimidating and overwhelming friend and foe alike. He was cold-hearted in the land of cutthroats.

"Success", he grimaced—now way too tired of performing.

'*Hamster-wheel Hass*', holding back tears now, needed distraction, the 'break' before breakdown or breakthrough. A diversion from the pain and constant inner turmoil, wrangling stomach tension, loud, unceasing, anguishing, weary thoughts haunting his head; emptied his soul. All this caused by seeking elusive, unsatisfying power, position, prestige, or money--more, more, and nauseatingly more.

Discerning the mountain that morning was difficult. Haziness between "success", and significance; business or just busy-ness, he remembered his family, hanging by a thread. Or, was it more like a tightening noose around his neck? His lifeline had been, he "did it all for them", now a cord of unraveling rope, potential failure. Where the greatest present would have been the gift of his presence, he could not grasp the irony.

Could she trust the integrity of that rope without hope? Marcie had become more calloused and alienated. Their two daughters slowly drifting away from Dad. Remembering those tightest of life's squeezes, from Daddy's girls; hugs that seemed to choke him with pure innocent love, clinging to the best in life. He missed them all.

His eyes slightly opened, he had been a Dominator not a Liberator, both at work and home. So much challenge with so little support buried those relationships. (GiANT) "Hang on" was the message he desperately wanted to send. Was this mountain an obstacle or a peek of hope?

From the cliffs of despair, an avalanche of overwhelming emotions and tears, exchanged as adrenalin stirred. Was this a fresh start, rejuvenating adventure at Base Camp? His past failures like that snowy windshield, could be a slate wiped clean. An opportunity to restart his climb.

For ages the mountains concealed foggy, elusive messages, mysteries hazy and hidden. Looking back at sea level, what could he see? Hass realized he was blind and clueless. Base Camp was ground zero for foundational preparation: apprentice training to conquer the mountain, beginning of the Death Zone, effectively and efficiently equipped, becoming acclimated in the process of dying.

Commonly people pursue their journey off-course, with poor, defective shallow anchors. "To safely crack the "rich" code, Hass needed to be equipped with only seven solid anchors. He would learn later, seven was the number of divine completeness, components of true prosperity from ancient times.

The most critical before the easy "What" and deceptive "Why", is finding "Who".

Enter Sherpa John, with a booming-famous, mountain-man voice, "Let's first consider 'Who', like any good English teacher would"! His keen intuition always drove climbers in the direction of True North. He believed with faith you can even move mountains, especially those not necessary to climb.

"Climb success is not dependent on altitude, but attitude. Humility and surrender means letting go of the ropes choking your life's vitality to reach greater heights", he continued.

It's all about priorities. Get 'Who" right first, sorting the Top 3 because a 3-cord strand is not easily broken: Love, Faith, and Hope: 'Who, What, and Why', then the other four anchors will fall in to place.

John explained, "Getting 'Who' right, because the greatest of these is Love, you'll meet the Great Sherpa-a Lifeline for all. As Sherpa John, I am a disciple of the Best, and a witness. I will decrease as you proceed, but He will increase in His role and guidance, and lead you into all Truth."

"So go ahead, Hass. Snatch one of the seven anchor-pebbles from my hand."

"Just for grins, I choose to start with 'Who' then!"

"You chose well." Sherpa John confirmed.

"I did. Who did I choose?"

"Yes, you did, young 'Grass Hopper.' Sherpa John chuckled. "You were previously consumed in clouds of 'What' you were doing, trying to justify it with 'Why'? Living by 'What' owns you, not 'Who' owns you, changes everything. This is the ultimate of life's questions. So, be honest with yourself this time."

"Further," Sherpa John continued, "If you own yourself, you are like all those who fail or fall short. But if you are owned by a Creator 'Who' designed you with purpose, the real 'What' you are living for becomes a higher mountain. You are climbing for a deeper meaning. "Climb deeper, not higher" becomes your 'Why', and battle cry."

"You must "Know Yourself to Lead Yourself." By confronting Hass with himself, Sherpa John mirrored for Hass what family, friends, coworkers saw; what it was like to be on the other side of him. (GiANT)

Celebrities, athletes, and yes, even CEOs commonly judged as achievers eventually see the fallout of their unhappiness in material, insubstantial 'things', and achievements. Most never figure out their mountain destiny. Most have no guide, no Sherpa.

"**Anchor #1** is 'Who' you chose", Sherpa John explains. "I prepare you for 'How' later. You will see 'The Way', the Truth, and the Life, after being introduced to the Great Sherpa, 'Who' is always there: FOR you Hass, on your side."

"Increase this Truth Hass, and you will clearly see. The Great Sherpa, as Provider offers a Lifeline, FOR your abundant life. This is the best news ever. Meaning and purpose from the Source of all good things. This Creator of all things, who owns the cattle on a thousand hills, and holds the stars in place is FOR you."

Like a Great Shepherd who seeks out and rescues the lost sheep caught on a dangerous cliff, he knows His sheep, and they hear and know His voice. The story from thousands of years ago, of the worlds' greatest rescue: The Great Sherpa demonstrated a proven servant's heart of sacrificial LOVE; and giving, He apparently died in the rescue mission of a single lost climber, "the legend of the lost" on a hill faraway.

His finished work and sacrificial death though settled it all…that we could rest or walk without heavy burdens in the light of His path for our journey. The greatest story ever told, sometimes never heard, He offers His constant companionship and partnership in life.

'Who' is worthy of our Trust for two good reasons: 1. He knows the plans He has for you, FOR your welfare to give you a future and a hope; and 2. The Great Sherpa overcame death, carrying the total avalanche, weight of the world's errors, saving a desperately lost climber who was injured and blinded from the fall. But consider 'Who' else?

"Caution young Hass." While you battle an ultimately defeated enemy, the villain seeks real victims to devour. He actively seeks to kill, steal, and destroy. Disasters, dangers: distractions, falls, thin air, avalanche, storms, crevasses, inferior cracks in the rich code. Historically, almost 300 have died on Everest, where they rest, but not in 'the rest' you seek for your life. Many are still, forever, buried there, hopes, memories and all. Out of 9,200 climbers, only 5,300 were successful. Almost half failed to reach the top.

No wonder Hass felt an unspeakable heaviness. This was the valley of the shadow of death.

The enemy seeks not all, but only those whom he may devour-the weak, lost and isolated. The solution: have all seven parameters solidly aligned. The battle of 'self-leadership' is most critical and comes first for all CEO's. The enemy-accuser can keep you caught in your past, unqualified for the mind-set and belief-set of a Victor.

The real self-leadership battle is for identity. You must know 'who' you are, and whose you are. That's why 'Who' is so important. Even the Great Sherpa was tested by the enemy, deceptively questioned alone in the wilderness about his identity. So, He understands our trials, temptations, pain, suffering, and challenges.

Hess, "He knows you intimately, and He can identify with all your challenges." He knows the number of hairs on your head, and loves you from Day 1, before the mountains were formed. There is nothing you have to prove. But 'Why' -**Anchor #2.**

As climber, sage Simon Sinek suggests "Start with Why" means knowing motives. Why climb, then, when you must go deeper to ascend?

"Hass, I challenge you to go seven "Why" levels deep, starting here at foundational Base Camp, asking 'why' each time to avoid blind spots on this dangerous slippery slope. Go for clarity of the peak: 'Why' positions, power and titles? Why money? Why riches? Blind spots are too dangerous on a mountain climb. Why this mountain?"

"Why ask why? Because we lie." Sherpa John explained. Elusive unexamined motivations, and the resulting failures make discipline a difficult 'process-mirror of the soul,' but is required to refine and test true motives.

"Know yourself to Lead yourself" up the mountain requires surrender to something better, not based on yourself, or your fragile efforts, frailties, and failures. (GiANT)

Self-leadership is never a given, but always a requirement leading yourself, especially before leading others. Your personal Sherpa may not always be there. Note that half the deaths on Everest are Sherpas. You must be able to lead yourself. Seven anchors rightly aligned within, living healthy from the inside out, reflects on others in relationships.

Others provide life-sustaining oxygen to your soul into life's thin air. The journey was never about you, and never for you, but for others. "Don't let your desired standard of living, with a steeper climb gradient and a deceptively-low peak, surpass the higher peak of relational deposits and quality of life you need to truly climb." (a peek from Joe Zerbo)

The early focus on 'What' before 'Why' put an invisible, undetectable ceiling on Hass's previous climb. With 'Who' and 'Why' in place for the climb; 'What' for a launch-point could now be surefooted on solid rock, **Anchor #3.**

Some climbers look down upon those who do not climb, staying true to their personal identity. When comparing to others who have their personal mountains to climb, or possibly descend, 'What' then becomes critical to quality of life, and abundant life.

Wisdom says all are created for purpose: with talents, skills, abilities, desires, dreams, passions, calling and destiny designed for greatness, for success, and for prosperity but reserved in personal exclusivity to 'What' they are called. Finding their unique mountain, the adventure of their journey, brings inner peace.

Delight yourself then in that Creator, and He will give you 'What' are the desires of your heart. He will plant those desires deep, that you must discover and pursue, and then grant those desires as you find Him the Source of all good things. Freely pursue, find riches, prosperity, and unrivaled unique, very personal success at 'What'-ever level then.

Moved by panic of not having enough, never satisfied or fulfilled, brings that smell, and 'secret fear' in your heart so real and rancid you can taste it. The constant tyranny of doubtfulness that no one around you suspects, puts you totally out-of-control, falling into the mountainous crevasses, the eternal abyss. The stakes are always too high for trappings of lack.

A quantity race to riches fails. Rare is the quality race of contentment. So do not consider 'What' before 'Why'. "Sherpas help you stay in one Peace. Choose Peace your new pursuit and a valid definition of 'What' your future success will be. But 'What Else'?

There will be obstacles that obscure vision, dangers, storms of adversity with white-out conditions, struggles, dream-stealers and dream-killers-the negative naysayers and distracting circumstances in life, failures requiring perseverance, perspective, and patience: floundering, lost, and temporary blurring, blinding blizzards of busy-ness. New faith perspective brings vision and hope through the storms.

Faith means believing, and is consistent belief, proven by action. Everyone says, "Seeing is believing". NO.

With new vision you learn that believing is seeing. When you begin to believe, you will see for the first time. New eyes, new perspective, and a fresh mountaintop vantage point will enable you to see more and grow in your faith. Not with your head, not logic and reason, but with your heart. With the heart climbers believe and achieve.

Leadership too is all about heart, and relationships. That is the 'What' of life, missing for many, but the essence of meaning and purpose, unfocused when there's not a pivotal, prioritized 'Who', 'Why' and 'What': which now points to 'Where'-**Anchor #4.**

The right place, the specific mountain calling is unique to everyone. According to ancient legends, mountains signify divinely inspired, constancy, spiritual transcendence, suggesting spiritual elevation to great exhilarating heights, a journey or pilgrimage. Stories describe the mysterious allure of the majestic mountain and man-pleasing production and results.

'Where'? There is only one path to 'Rich' not many paths. Riches can blind an oblivious pursuit to bottomless crevasse, a crack to an unending fall. Sherpa John threw the ultimate lifeline, a rescue rope, to hang Hass's last hope, letting go of past dead ends. The right mountain rope with all seven anchors aligned, Hass could now navigate to overcome obstacles even after being detoured from distractions, delusions, and disasters.

'Where'-ever you happen to be today, geographically and emotionally, spiritually, and physically the Great Sherpa finds you, meets you. John reminded Hass, "He calls out to you and guides you safely home from your starting point."

From EveRest that place for the weary that you were seeking, 'Where' you could place your hope, and finally rest--right place, and yes, the right time, **Anchor #5**...

'When'? Now is the time. The "fierce urgency of now" calls for action not just intellectual assent and talk. (Reverend Dr. Martin Luther King) Timing in the context of 'Who' and 'Why' doing 'What', 'Where' and now 'When'. Yes, NOW.

Leaders recognize the mountainside gravity of time. Leaders are lifelong learners who actively leave and live a legacy. Learning from the past, living in the present, longing for their amazing future, leaders ACT.

Temporal is just what we see, that which does not last. However, the invisible things are eternal. Why waste time on what passes away, things, riches, time itself. Invest in the eternal, where time is of no consequence. The future is not constrained by time.

Change your mountain Everest, to "ForEveRest". Rename and redefine your mountain as you rewrite, and re-right your story to leave a lasting legacy. Tested and true, timeless principles: yesterday, today, and tomorrow. Past present and future, the Great Sherpa is always the same. A sure foundation allows forever rest, as the Anchor holds.

Not slalom pursuing a downhill endless furious race: but seeking Shalom, a restful peace that passes understanding, beyond comprehension. But 'How'? **Anchor #6.**

Shalom describes peace in every dimension; complete well-being, physical, mental, emotional, psychological, social, and spiritual, flowing from all of Hass's relationships being put right—with God and others, in harmony, health, wholeness, prosperity, and tranquility.

Live better for others by dying to self sooner, even more fully alive, resting in peace. Things ('What') like being in the right place ('Where'), at the right time ('When'), for the right reasons ('Why'): 'Who' better than a Great Sherpa who has seen it all, knows it all, has experienced 'How' including your pain and challenges. And 'To what extent'? No limits: **Anchor #7.**

Hass moved from Base Camp Everest to Mt Foreverest for the legacy of his life. He chose the highest and deepest of callings, meaning Foreverestmore. Hass found no limits while recognizing his new Source, Course and Force for a life of both significance and success with all seven anchors synergistically aligned.

Champion now, instead of business CEO, of his unique journey to self-discovery, co-laboring, and coordinating with the Creator for Marcie and the girls, to serve and guide others, his newfound destiny, becoming a Sherpa for them all, giving by serving, and remembering unmistakably FOR others.

Not Mt. Everest; but Foreverest. New perspective beyond vast, hopeless mountains, no obstacles 'insight'! The Great Sherpa is able to do immeasurably more than all one asks or imagines, according to his power that is at work within to achieve heights beyond imagination for Hass.

Driver John announced the awakening. "We're here boss…in one peace".

Hass declared with a wink and a nod. "Yes, we are!", returning from his mulligan-mountaintop experience.

Previously thinking he was scaling a mountain, he was digging a hole, a bottomless canyon. A death spiral on a senseless journey of a thousand unnamed mountains.

Then came a personal mountain journey of self-discovery to achieve a remarkable peace. The wealth, prosperity Hess sought to crack the 'Real Rich Code' of wealth, not dollars, prestige, and title, was concealed-now revealed as shalom-rest.

Recognizing that everyone is in the process of dying like Hass at Everest's Base Camp, death became a spiritual and leadership life-growth process.

Not about doing, but being and becoming, character is that higher calling. 'Be'-ing is more important than 'Do'-ing. And 'Do-ing is more effective when 'Be-ing' with true character. A transformational turning point: that soaring butterfly moment, no longer a grasshopper, or caterpillar, now climbing for a higher purpose and calling, with deeper meaning. Powerful beyond compare.

He surrendered living for self, to living FOR others. By arriving at the 'end-of-me' he left behind his greatest enemy. Like ancient Pogo before, "He met the enemy, and he is me."

Since Everest and now Foreverestmore Hass Gropper has been…

…dying through the greatest adventure ever lived to achieve a legacy he could never attain on his own. He is "Cracking the Rich Code on Everest for a Better More Majestic Mountain" on Foreverest.

REFERENCES

GiANT Worldwide.

"Half Time", Bob Buford, 1997.

"Start with Why", Simon Sinek, 2009.

"The Grace Revolution." Joseph Prince, 2015.

The Holy Bible.

***

Dr. Tom Heemstra, Lt.Col. USAF Retired

CEO, MACH 5 Leadership Solutions, Executive Coaching & Consulting

***

To contact Tom:

drtom@mach5ls.com Cell (865) 585-0047, Please leave a voicemail message

Linked In: linkedin.com/in/dr-tom-heemstra-ltcol-ret-6246b8a

Facebook: https://facebook.com/tom.heemstra1

or Twitter: Tom Heemstra@HeemstraTom

or: TomHeemstraSuccess.com

# Shahnaz Ghafoor

Shahnaz Ghafoor's passion for creativity was fostered at a young age by her mother – a novice interior decorator, and her father - an artist before he became an engineer and, ultimately, a businessman. A self-made couple that emigrated to the U.S. in the 80's, Shahnaz's parents further taught her business strategies from a very young age, earning her the advantage of serving on a Board of Directors as a mere teenager. With degrees in advertising, economics and interior design, Shahnaz melded her diverse background into an effective growth strategy as a young entrepreneur.

As President/Founder of Silver Chase Design – Art & Interiors, Shahnaz's cutting-edge ideas have earned her numerous honors, including the Houston Business Journal's *40 Under 40* and *Women Who Mean Business*. While her personal model to success centers on a willingness to push herself beyond standards and limitations, it is her commitment to her clients' success that has been instrumental to the success of her designs.

In her private time, when she is not picking up stray animals to "grow [her] farm", Shahnaz stays heavily involved in the local community. Whether she is dressing up as a snow queen for patients at a local children's hospital, mentoring creative-minded entrepreneurs at seminars or creating new branding strategies for a non-profit, she exhibits kindness and devotion in all avenues of life.

## It's Not Luck

***By Shahnaz Ghafoor***

Is there truly a secret to success? Could it just be some people's luck? They had advantages I didn't have, right? The answer to questions such as these is always a resounding, "No!"

When it comes to success, lack of funding, being underqualified, being overqualified, a weak economy, personal circumstances, discrimination, nepotism – any of these factors can alter your life overnight, without your permission and without giving you a chance to brace yourself. We all have a backstory. A series of successive events which occurred in an almost orchestrated manner to get us to the moment that built us up, broke us down and then forced us to be here…Writing this chapter…Reading this book. The hardest part about being "here" is that something has likely gone wrong – life has been disrupted! What now?

Five years ago, I went from being one of the best-known art directors in corporate interior design to being jobless in a world that seemed to have changed without me - without *my* permission and without giving *me* a chance to brace myself. You may not relate to my profession, but you could conceivably picture yourself in a relatable circumstance. When we compare my journey to yours, I am certain there will be similarities. Some common ground where we connect with each other in an inexplicable way, even though we never crossed paths.

Despite our individualities, the general human population shares categorical similarities. Perhaps the most common similarity is, simply, that we work. Whether it is working in a factory or a Fortune 500 company, whether it is designing an app or a patent, whether it is being a homemaker or an executive, we are all working to fill necessary roles in a functional society. The daily routine gives us purpose which, in turn, gives us a sense of security because we are prepared for what is to come the next day. So, one day, if you wake up and you no longer have that job that you loved, or hated, you have ultimately lost your purpose. That sudden loss of the sense of security is where our similarities converge, no matter how different we may be. That is the moment when you can hear a stranger's story, such as this, and relate to it on a highly personal level.

There are many avenues that can be taken to tell a singular story: dramatic narrative, technical step-by-step, strategic methodology, or a juicy tell-all. I am not the only person to have faced disappointment and I am also not the only success story out there, so I obsessed over how to make this meaningful to someone motivated to seek positive direction in life. Opening-up about professional matters can be tricky. It is possible to share too much and, sometimes, too little. Like many others, I often internalize personal struggles because I am a strong person, and I do not want to appear weak or emotional. However, if you have the courage to start anew, I can reciprocate by sharing the grit and glory of what transpired *between* my successes - that suspenseful limbo between *what is* and *what could be.*

## CONFIDENCE

I cannot emphasize enough, the importance of *not* festering on the sad story that has inspired you to search for fresh insight. You will never hear me talk about why I had to leave a job that I actually loved because it is irrelevant to my current success. The past is an amazing learning tool, but the undesirable aspects that are encountered on occasion are hardly something to dwell on if you want to succeed and be happy. Save your energy from negative thoughts and emotions of the past because, in the absence of knowing what comes next, your mind is about to go through the wringer.

When I left my job, I started off calm and optimistic. The very first thing I did to tackle the situation head-on was absolutely nothing. For me, after more than a decade of having a highly focused goal, the most difficult task was refocusing on a new goal, mostly because I did not have one. I had to abandon a paved path without a detour and all I knew is that any road ahead would be bumpy. So, in the absence of purpose, I spent a month on my couch watching movies with my latest rescue animal sitting on my stomach. Her favorite, in case you were wondering, was Alice in Wonderland. Don't worry, this was not an example of hitting rock bottom. This was a detox stage and, possibly, the most important event of the aftermath because it was a sliver of time where I was able to clear my mind of accrued negativity and re-energize myself for the upcoming mental battle (which I did not know was coming).

Despite being a person that never lacked self-confidence, not having a job compromised my self-worth. As reality settled in, my emotions were simple - I felt destroyed. In my early career, I was often perceived as a wild card because my ideas appeared too progressive for the time. People knew I *could* do amazing things, but the question was, "*Will* she do amazing things?" Being successful answered that question for everyone and it validated me as a person. While I was working, I had a daily routine that provided a sense of security. I had somewhere to be every morning, people needed me, I loved my projects and I got a paycheck. These things somehow made me relevant. Suddenly, without a job, I felt like I was eyeballs deep in an imaginary dumpster, trying to find value within myself, yet all I kept finding was day old noodles. In the same scenario, my "self" worth was contingent upon someone else telling me that I was good enough - for them…for their company. Oh, the irony!

My initial strategy was to seek a conservative alternative out of my situation - in other words, find another job quickly. I was a highly educated person with a reputation for being clever and aggressive. People liked me and I was a huge asset to a company's bottom line, so it made sense that I had plenty of suitors once I finally got off the sofa (or climbed out the dumpster, depending on which scenario you are following). That rush you get from prospective employers racing to get to you first was invigorating, but I quickly ended up feeling worse than I did when I was simply feeling bad about myself. How is that even possible? What was going on?

I am a huge proponent of profitability, but capitalism seemed to be at its finest that year. Every interviewer was someone probing me about how I could make them rich overnight. Is "overnight" even an appropriate interview term? I could practically see it in their eyes – lemons, cherries, jokers and dollar signs spinning round-and-round like a slot machine, and I better promise a jackpot.

My favorite dialogue went something like this:

A man asked, "Why should I hire you if you can't guarantee me a profit of $1 million before the end of the year?" Mind you, it was already May.

I replied, "If $1 million was a realistic possibility before the end of the year, why would I make it for you and not myself?"

My self-worth seemed irrelevant in exchange for what I could do for someone's net worth. Perhaps I should have been flattered, but the entire process felt rather offensive. Ultimately, I cycled back to my good old sofa, contemplating what I truly wanted for myself. *Wanted*, not needed! And what I wanted was to give the finger to a whole lot of people. But right after that, I wanted to humanize the workplace again. I wanted to go back to doing exactly what I love yet make it better by fueling constructive change in the socio-economic culture by creating a gratifying work environment and, of course, make money doing it...Overnight, if necessary.

## CAPITAL

My biggest roadblock, one which stifles the ambitions of many, was money. The bottom line is that I did not plan for not having a job and, without an income or collateral, no financial institution was willing to invest in me to start a business. Although I had the plan and the know-how, I had zero capital. Not a dollar to spare! Without money, you would think that a person could not possibly build a business, but that simply did not end up being the case.

One of the keys to success is resourcefulness. Today's economy is dense with resources that are quite literally at our fingertips, thanks to the internet. Nearly everyone has, or has access to, a computer or a smart phone. With an abundance of competition just a click away, e-commerce is eager for you to give it a chance so you will often see "Free 30-Day Trial" sprawled across thousands of websites for service-oriented and product-based businesses. I leveraged those four little words to buy myself some time - thirty days, to be exact! With thirty days to create an empire, I locked myself down over a weekend and started structuring the foundation of a viable business. Starting with the fundamentals, I built a website, downloaded state documents to be filed, created templates for day-to-day operations, designed business cards and brushed up on essential software.

Although I will forever continue to learn and evolve, in that moment, I learned enough to get myself to next step.

According to the U.S. Bureau of Labor Statistics, about twenty percent of businesses fail in their first year and about fifty percent fail by year five. The risk of disappointment was a definite possibility and so was the lack of sleep. I think my longest bout of restlessness was four nights in a row – long enough to feel delirious, but not quite long enough to start hallucinating. Stress seemed to be a lingering nuisance, but only because of the projected fear of the future. When I compartmentalized into smaller time frames, everything became manageable, and I found benefit in celebrating the small victories.

My first completed project only earned nine hundred dollars. That does not sound like a lot of money, but you must look at the big picture in perspective. I started with zero capital and had only thirty days to produce any amount of income to pay for the infrastructure that I set-up on a trial basis! Even though I had considerable projects on the books (further explained in the next section), the lead times were longer and could not address my immediate financial needs. Used strategically, nine hundred dollars was more than I needed to fill the gap.

My tactics were not exactly a gamble, but the game I was playing was not for the faint of heart. Still, the pay-out exceeded my dreams. Banks regularly approach me now to conduct business and, while I see that as another small victory, my greatest accomplishment will remain the aspiration to pursue affirmative change regardless of the circumstances. In other words, I gave it a shot! Not every start-up has investors or financial support, but there are certainly resources available to every entrepreneur, if they have the determination to fight for designing the life they want to live.

**CONNECTIONS**

It takes a lot to advance in a competitive market and at the core of it is the network of connections that encourages you and the growth of your business. Imagine throwing a party. You send out invitations, put out tons of food and drink, decorate your venue from top to bottom, and even hire a DJ. It looks like you are ready to go, except, it is not a party unless and until people show up. Every person that shows up is part of your network and their involvement interconnects your intentions to your success.

There is a popular belief that making *new* connections is essential to the growth of a business, so professionals from every industry flock to networking events with business cards in hand, hoping to infiltrate new markets and find the next lead. Afterall, it makes sense. Get your name out there, let people recognize your face, and exchange ideas with a fresh stock of motivated individuals. There is absolute value to generating new business by forming new connections. The process itself can be slow in producing results, but it keeps you relevant. Some people may even advise that you need to start networking before initiating a business plan in order to build a viable business. This is where I feel the model is flawed. Although making new connections is valuable, *managing existing connections* will be most integral to the foundation of your business.

My business grew very quickly and very publicly. Part of it was an effective marketing strategy, but there was a second determining factor, and that was the contribution made by my existing connections. In the absence of money or magical fairy dust, I could not possibly produce product, staff projects, or provide services to clients if I did not have a system of supporters. In fact, my company would not exist today, had it not been for a business opportunity brought forth by a meaningful relationship that resulted from a sustainable connection.

One afternoon in June, I received a message from an old client. It read, "I have a new project. When can you come by?" This was one of my favorite clients so, from my trusted sofa, I explained that I no longer worked…anywhere…and referred them to a former colleague that could assist. A few weeks later, the same client sent another message. "Where have you landed? You need to work on this project." Out of loyalty, I scheduled a meeting with my client and shared an honest conversation with them about my abilities (I am the best at what I do) and limitations (there was no way little old me could get past the red tape to be a contractor for such a big corporation). To my surprise, as a small group of us stood in the middle of a room, two women in the group started a dialogue with each other about how to navigate me through the system. They divided a task list, made the necessary calls and, by the time I pulled up to my driveway that day, I was relevant again. Perhaps because I was jaded by the devaluation that I encountered in the interviewing process, it had not occurred to me that, in the professional relationships I had formed over the years, there was positive value being placed on me as an individual. People with no agenda simply appreciated my work ethic and wanted to help.

If you did things right, you started forming meaningful relationships from the first day of your first job and from every walk of life. Before you grow, you must *exist*, so being connected to a positive group of contributors establishes your baseline and inevitably leads to new opportunities and facilitates overall success. For growth, a valuable connection is not just a prospective client. It is the client from way back when that gives you a chance. It is the vendor that extends a line of credit when a financial institution is not willing. It is an old co-worker who volunteers services to design your company logo. It is a colleague that works projects with you when you are understaffed. It is the friend that insists, "You can do this," when you doubt yourself. By default, these people have become your trusted mentors, partners, counselors and advisors. You are not a one-man-show because you already have a team.

Although there are hundreds of factors that cannot be controlled in your career path, success comes from maintaining focus on the fact that only you have ownership of your personal strength and determination. No success story was ever written without a door shut in the face or numerous sleepless nights. You have to check-in with yourself daily to maintain the balance between being happy and being successful. I rely on persistence, despite difficulty or delay because, without it, my fight does not go on and my story, which has turned into an adventure, does not continue.

After a pretty entertaining journey involving a sofa and a black cat, a simple realization emerged - I *am* the best at what I do! I lost a job, not myself! I design my own "luck", so I repositioned myself for success and founded Silver Chase Design – Art & Interiors. My new job as president of this creative agency keeps me involved in absolutely every invigorating and annoying facet of the business. "I wear many hats," as the saying goes. That sounds like a fashion faux pas, but as a business strategy, it keeps me actively engaged to inspire new ideas and enthusiasm from within my organization so that we may dare to innovate new standards in interior aesthetics for an ever-evolving corporate community.

Being an entrepreneur gives you creative license to decide what you take away from each day. When I wake up, I get to manage designs for a sixty-feet wide outdoor sculpture one day and create VIP cyber lounges for executives the next day. By the third day, I am researching the local heritage of a historical city to curate a custom designed art program. Healthcare, hospitality, finance, oil and gas, non-profit…each client culture allows me to delve into something excitingly different from the perspective of branded art and interior design.

In my personal aspirations and professional ambitions, my take-away is not to think outside the box because, quite frankly, everyone is doing that. I think of what I can do *with* the box.

***

To contact Shahnaz:

www.silverchasedesign.com

SG@silverchasedesign.com

http://www.silverchasedesign.com/connect

https://www.instagram.com/silverchasedesign/

https://www.linkedin.com/in/shahnaz-ghafoor-056a3b16

## Rory Douglas

Rory Douglas is a Best-Selling Author, Financial Educator and High Performance Life Coach. He was born in Chicago, IL and raised in Los Angeles CA. Moving to Los Angeles, Douglas made his mark in the music industry by developing his company, RKD Music & Talent Management, with his former law partner Joseph Gellman.

For the next 20 years, Douglas led the way for artists and talent to excel in the music industry. He is a Platinum and Gold Record Selling Executive Producer and has furnished his music catalog to several hit films. Douglas is a spokesman for several National Educational Seminars, Conferences, Colleges and Universities. He has also been Keynote Speaker at organizations such as the South California Women's Conference and the Veterans Administration to name a couple.

Douglas is also Author of books like **"Artificial Intelligence"**, **"The Power to Get Wealth: No Money Required"** and the Best-Selling book **"Fear to Freedom "**. He has quickly become a force in the financial industry as well as a leading authority on retirement planning as a Financial Educator and Retirement Specialist. His focus is uplifting his audience to a powerful, productive new mindset of financial freedom.

Douglas is on a National Financial Literacy Campaign to educate 1 Million families by year 2021. His firm, Aqua Financial Center, is located in Encino CA.

## The Money Game: Millennial Makeover

***By Rory Douglas***

There is a Grave Epidemic that is going on in America today. The average American is at least one to two paychecks away from being homeless; one in three are in debt. The average American cannot handle a $400 emergency and millennials have zero savings.

Millennials having zero savings is very troubling. If this matter is not addressed immediately, the future seems very unfavorable. Also known as Generation Y, millennials are the demographic cohort following Generation X and preceding Generation Z. Researchers and popular media use the early 1980's to the early 2000's as ending birth years, with 1981 to 1996 being a widely accepted definition.

A millennial makeover is when someone does not see their full potential. They need someone else to come in and show them the way. According to recent surveys, North American's are facing serious financial challenges. Thirty-three percent, or more than 77-million Americans don't pay their bills on time. Thirty-nine percent carry credit card debt from month to month. Only 59% percent of adults say they have savings. Worse, more than half now think it's acceptable to default on their mortgage if they can't afford to pay.

Many of us don't wait to become a statistic to know that we're in trouble. These problems are all around us. They happen to be in our own families and in that of our friends. It's ironic that we live in one of the wealthiest countries in the world, but we always have money problems. We can work hard all of our lives but retire poor. So much effort we put into providing a bright future for our kids just to see them finish college buried in debt.

Debt becomes a way of life. Nobody teaches us how to manage our money in school. Financial issues are not often discussed; financial products are not always explained. Most people have trouble balancing their own check books and reading a financial statement. Credit cards are used daily without a clear understanding of hidden charges. We contribute to our retirement plans with the hope that someone else will grow it. People don't plan to fail; they just fail to have a plan.

The millennials must get prepared for a new industry. Artificial intelligence will create major job displacements. Trouble is on the horizon. Today, we go into the supermarket, bank, airport, parking lots, and we see machines. Students must be aware of the dangers and pitfalls that lie ahead.

According to the McKinsey Global Institute, up to 800-million global workers will lose their jobs by 2030 and be replaced by robotic automation. Some of the jobs that will soon become extinct are newspaper workers, travel agents, radio jockeys, bank tellers, truck drivers and manufacturing workers.

Financial literacy is a must. Millennials must learn how to take care of their financial selves or prepare to suffer the consequences. Vast amounts of millennials are training for a career that is fading away as a new industry is coming in. It is imperative that the information that is right under the noses of millennials are brought to their attention. It's just like a tree, if you don't like the fruit that the tree produces, don't get mad at the fruit, get mad at the root.

Although education is key, millennials must allow their imaginations to run wild and pursue their purpose through entrepreneurship and creativity. Millennials must get their SHIFT together and quickly. This new industry requires a new mindset. Independence and entrepreneurism are needed like never before. Today in America, a new home-based business is started every twelve-seconds. Did you know that home-based businesses earn $427-billion a year? It is estimated that in the United States, there are 38-million home-based businesses. Seventy percent of home-based businesses succeed within three years vs regular businesses. Forty-four percent of home-based businesses are started for under $5,000. Twenty percent of home-based businesses make $100,000 to $500,000 a year. Eighty-five percent of Americans are dissatisfied with their job. Over 70% of Americans would prefer to be self-employed.

Now it's time for millennials to get into the money game and crack the rich code. Let's start with the real rate of return on our money. The average major bank in America gives us, on average, about a minus one percent of interest on a checking or savings account. We have more than 13-trillion-dollars sitting in United States banks earning less than 1% interest. Inflation is about 3.5%. For example, if you saved $100 at 3% interest that would yield you $103.00. The taxes on $103.00 is about 75 cents. Net after taxes is $102.25. The inflation is $3.50. The actual return is $98.75, so you lose.

Would you rather pay $0.75 or $3.50? Quite naturally you would rather pay $0.75 but I have news for you, we pay both. It's not the taxes that's killing us, it's inflation, which I call the silent killer. We must have at least 5% or greater interest to beat taxes and inflation.

The second component is The Rule of 72 and compounding interest. The Rule of 72 is used by all banking institutions and finance companies. The Rule of 72 can work for you or against you. It works for you if you are receiving the interest. However, if you are paying the interest, like a credit card, it works against you.

Want this formula? Simply take the number 72 and divide it into any rate of return. That tells you how long it takes to double your money. The two above statements are examples of the failure of the educational system. Schools do not teach us how to sell, think, negotiate, face our failures, invest our money, find our passion, make an impact, start a business, or how to communicate well.

In fact, the conditions of the millennials today have a substantial resemblance to the Great Depression. For example, during the great depression, Americans suffered a massive job loss, lack of opportunity, collapse of major job industries, and collapse of the stock market. These conditions left Americans with scarce liquidity and very little to transfer to the succeeding generation. Americans had to use life insurance as a form of wealth transformation.

Wealth transformation is the transfer of wealth or assets to beneficiaries upon the death of the owner through financial planning. These strategies often include wills, estate planning, life insurance, or trusts. Although today's conditions in America are polar opposite of that during the Great Depression, due to financial illiteracy and the millennials having zero savings, they must use the same resources as did their predecessors for financial freedom. Today's society is filled with booming industries, technological advancements, social media, and abundant opportunities. Unfortunately, millennials have no form of wealth transformation.

Frankly, they have nothing to transfer. If millennials don't shift their thinking, perilous times lie ahead.

I believe today's millennials are the finest that America has yet to see. They are fearless, creative, resourceful and highly educated. They simply need to crack the rich code by understanding the importance of financial literacy and entrepreneurism. If they do, they will be unstoppable, and the future looks very promising.

Take a look at some of the top industries and who's leading the way. For example, Mark Zuckerberg of Facebook, Travis Kalanick and Garrett Camp of Uber, Brian Chesky of Airbnb, Ben Silbermann and Evan Sharp of Pinterest, Adam D'Angelo of Quora, Mike Krieger and Kevin Systrom of Instagram and Sean Rad of Tinder to name a few. The millennials above have managed to disrupt and revolutionize the way we approach travel, socializing and even dating. They are prime examples of what happens when millennials think outside of the box.

Now that we all are motivated after reading that list, I have a few suggestions for millennials to take while they are encompassing their entrepreneurial ventures: They must establish a solid foundation (i.e., having a form of wealth transformation such as life insurance). They must establish a debt management plan (i.e. raising their credit score). They must apply the "10/20 Rule" (They need at least ten-times their monthly expenses saved up for an emergency and at least twenty-times their yearly salary to retire). Remember, retirement has nothing to do with your age. You can retire at 18-years-old if you're financially secure. Lastly, once the foundation is secure, they can invest. Millennials today invest first, save last, and have no foundation. Furthermore, millennials have to transition from flat interest to compounding interest, and they must learn about the three forms of taxes to get ahead.

The three forms of taxes are tax now, tax later, and tax advantage. The average American is in the tax now category which are checking accounts, savings accounts, CD's, stocks and mutual funds. Following that is the tax later category which are 401k's, IRA's, annuities and pensions. We must get into the tax advantage (tax free) category which are Roth IRA's, college savings plans, municipal bonds, health savings accounts and life insurance. We can no longer have a champagne taste with a beer budget.

I would encourage millennials to take full advantage of the unlimited opportunities that are available today. Always remember that opportunity and access is greater than money. We have to remove ourselves from the mentality of trading time for money and the rat race of the 9-5. Start thriving as opposed to surviving. Don't be discouraged as success is often found in a pile of mistakes. Do not allow your circumstances to shrink your dreams and most certainly do not allow fear to rob you of your destiny. If millennials combine their faith, belief and passion with their education, financial literacy, and entrepreneurism, they will have money for a lifetime and not a lunch time.

***

To contact Rory:

www.RoryDouglas.net

info@rorydouglas.net

Phone: (310) 712-1980

Instagram: RorykDouglas

Facebook: OfficialRoryDouglas

Youtube: OfficialRoryDouglas

## Kate Miller

Kate Miller is an entrepreneur, world traveler, freelance writer and yoga teacher. She left her corporate job in 2017 to start Kate Rae Digital, a social media consulting and content agency. In her first year Kate doubled her income and has seen continued year-over-year growth. Kate and her team help brands and companies use social media to connect in meaningful ways with their audience. She is passionate about creating a work environment where both employees and clients find value in their work, reach goals, and maintain a rewarding work/life balance.

Kate also has a yoga, mindfulness, and retreat business called Lets Really Live. She creates safe spaces for people to explore yoga and find inner joy. She has been asked to speak at events and conferences about her experiences, social media and mindset. She also writes for several online outlets and has been quoted in national publications.

Without any formal business background, Kate credits her success to mindset, experiences and strong network. She is currently working on launching an e-commerce business and has several other projects in the works. Kate is a dreamer, curious and always up for a challenge.

Kate is based in Minnesota and Florida, but her business is remote, so she spends much of her time exploring the world. Kate collects cookbooks from everywhere she travels and hopes to write one soon. She enjoys hosting people around her table, running, reading, creating things, sewing, and sunsets.

## Thinking Like an Entrepreneur

***By: Kate Miller***

When someone asks where you want to go to dinner, how do you answer? Your response could play an important part in your success as an entrepreneur. How many times did you just question your response? Your thought process is another key factor in your journey. The path to success requires constantly adapting, making hard decisions and overcoming adversity. Thinking like an entrepreneur is what divides those who go after their dreams and those who spend a lifetime talking about it. Everyone has a different path to entrepreneurship, but it all comes down to one word – mindset.

In the summer of 2017, I bought a house, quit my well-paying corporate job, and started a business. At the time I didn't have a website or business card. In the first year I doubled my salary and shortly after hired my first employee. Less than three years later I'm still expanding and have yet to write a business plan. While conventional wisdom wouldn't recommend this approach, it's why I have found success. I always knew I wanted to be a business owner, but I didn't go into 2017 thinking that would be the year. However, I knew the timing would never be perfect so when an opportunity presented itself, I jumped all in. When people ask me how I did it, I tell them mindset.

### DON'T OVERTHINK IT

The biggest obstacle most entrepreneurs have to overcome is themselves. How many times have you asked to pick someone's brain over coffee or taken an online course to learn just one more thing? How many times have you edited your website or asked for one more opinion before launching? Don't get me wrong, learning and networking are an important part of being an entrepreneur. However there comes a day where it's time to stop thinking so much and just take the leap. Ask yourself if that day is today. My guess is that it's time. Time to go after what you want.

I regularly get asked to sit down with people who are thinking about starting a business. They talk about how their logo isn't perfect or list out all the risks associated with their dream. I always try to shift the conversation from negative to positive. Let's talk about why the logo is ready instead of what's wrong with it. Or let's focus on the rewards that can come from going after their dream instead of the risk. We are human. We are built to see risks and can talk ourselves out of just about anything. If you want to get out of the dreaming phase and into being an entrepreneur faster, surround yourself with yes people. We already know why something might not work, find the people who will help you see how it can work. Then don't overthink it. Shift your mindset from what if to I'm ready.

**BE DECISIVE**

This brings us back to my first question. When someone asks where you want to go to dinner, how do you answer? If you know what you want without hesitation, you're thinking like an entrepreneur. Being decisive is a daily character trait of success. When you're first getting started, everything is your choice. Brand colors, financial decisions, tagline, website copy, you are responsible for each decision. As your business grows, the decisions do too. Eventually you're making decisions about who to hire, investments, and growth. Without a decisive mindset, you could quickly find yourself in decision fatigue.

Make decision-making easier by getting clear on what you want, who you are, and where you are going. Even if you're like me and don't have a business plan (yet!), take some time to lay out your goals and vision. Line up each decision with your bigger picture. When you're thrown a curveball, and you will be thrown one, a clear vision will help you find a clear answer.

Being decisive in your yes and no will also play a key role in your success. As you grow as an entrepreneur you'll be presented with many opportunities. It can be easy to say yes to everything and eventually lose track of your own plan. When people extend invites, partnership deals, or other opportunities, ask yourself if it's 100% aligned with your vision. If it's not, right now might not be the time.

**ASK FOR HELP**

This is not to be confused with point one – overthinking. Asking for help is about knowing you don't have to do everything yourself. Being an entrepreneur can be a time-consuming and at times a lonely journey. The first year I had my business I'm pretty sure I didn't turn on the TV and I rarely saw friends and family. I worked through every vacation and let the plants in my house die. In year two, I got better. I started asking for help. Eventually, I hired.

Asking for help isn't always easy, especially when you own a business. We dream up an idea, put our heart and soul into, and hold it close. But without help, there is not growth. Start by getting connected to other business owners and exchanging ideas. Find out how they manage productivity and what best practices they've learned. Reach out to friends and family to ask for help with personal tasks that may be falling behind. For the past three years my mom regularly visits my house to break down and recycle boxes. It may seem small, but without her I wouldn't be able to walk into my garage.

And finally, figure out where you should hire. Remember time is money. Determine your hourly rate and take a look at where you could free up time to be more profitable. For example, if you live somewhere it snows, is it a good use of your time to take a few hours a day to shovel? Chances are you can hire someone at an affordable price to shovel while you continue working and bill out at a much higher rate. Related to your business, there are many experts who can do the things you're trying to learn on Google. Instead of spending hours teaching yourself Search Engine Optimization, you'll get a better return on your time and results, by hiring someone who is already an expert. Start with freelancers or consultants and as your business grows, start to hire the right full-time people for your team. If you aren't investing in your business, how can you expect others to do the same?

## ESTABLISH HABITS

One of the best investments I made was hiring a business coach who taught me the importance of habits. Without the constraints of a traditional 9 – 5, an entrepreneur's day can be unpredictable. Establishing habits helps retain structure and increase productivity. Most importantly, habits can reduce stress and keep you aligned with what's important in your life. In fact, I recommend starting there. Start with habits that bring you personal joy and well-being. There is a reason the flight attendant tells us to put our own air mask on before someone else's. If you don't take care of yourself first, it's hard to take care of others. Whatever your thing is – working out, yoga, meditation, reading – build that into your weekly calendar first. Make it a habit and stick to it, even when things get busy. If you have to sacrifice a meeting for your daily run, it will be worth it. You'll be a better entrepreneur when you take care of yourself.

Professional habits will also help lead to success. Start with one or two habits and do them well. The fastest way to fail on habits is to take on too many, too soon. Write down your habit, establish the process, and give yourself a reward. It can be as simple as doing billing every Friday at noon and rewarding yourself with an afternoon tea. Once that habit becomes routine, start to build in new habits. Eventually your habits become a lifestyle.

## CREATE CLEAR BOUNDARIES

Habits and boundaries go hand-in-hand. You're the boss. You set the boundaries. If one of your morning habits is a workout, maybe that means no email before 8 am. If meetings on Fridays don't serve you best, then you don't have to have them. The mindset here is getting clear on what you need to be most successful and being OK with saying no. You don't clock in and out of being an entrepreneur. It's a 24-hour, 365-day job if you let it. But that's the joy of job, the choice is yours. You control your life; life doesn't control you.

Boundaries can come in all forms. Based on values, your habits, and personal goals, create clear boundaries. Just like habits, start with your personal boundaries. What do you need on a personal level to succeed as an entrepreneur? Consider intellectual, emotional and spiritual beliefs. You are entitled to your own thoughts and opinions. Give yourself permission to determine what this is for you. Next take a look at your professional boundaries. This can start with the way you set up your contracts. Consider payment terms, rush fees, and meeting etiquette. Another professional boundary are the types of projects or events you say yes to. If you don't feel aligned with a brand or person, you get to make the choice to say no.

Establishing boundaries can be one of the hardest transitions from corporate America to entrepreneurship. In a traditional job, someone tells you what time to arrive at work, how much you'll be paid, what your role is, and how many vacation days you get. As an entrepreneur, those guidelines are all gone. It took months before I didn't feel guilty about ending my day at 2 pm or taking a three-hour lunch. This goes back to being decisive. Decide what you need and make that your new standard.

## EMBRACE FAILURE

Did you know there are companies funding projects to help start-ups fail faster? You read that right. Fail faster. Failure in entrepreneurship can be a positive thing. This requires a shift in mindset. You're no longer in a culture of fear, you're in a culture of opportunity. Each failure is a lesson. Each negative response is feedback. Each setback leads to a step forward. Find a process of trial and error and start learning. Get comfortable with failing and you'll find success.

Embracing failure starts with seeing opportunity in everything. If your new design has a flaw, this just became your greatest strength. Don't look at the flaw as a negative, embrace it as a way to evolve the product to be even better. Maybe through the process you'll find that flaw applies to other companies and a new revenue stream could be to help them solve it too. An entrepreneur doesn't complain about an app not doing what they want, they start to look for ways to make a better app. Start to have fun with failure and see the opportunities it can create.

This shift in mindset goes back to point one again. Don't overthink it. Instead of waiting for everything to be perfect, put your product or service out there. Social media can be a great place to soft launch and get real-time feedback on the ways you can strengthen your offering. Start a private Facebook group or crowdsource feedback on Twitter, and let your audience be part of the journey. Not only does this get you to market faster, it can also help build real, authentic connections with your customers before launch.

## BE OPEN TO CHANGE

Plans are great but don't get too attached. The road to entrepreneurship can be twisted, complicated, and filled with dead ends. Create a clear vision but be open to change along the way. Tying into failure, things won't always go as planned. Contracts will change, shipments will be delayed, and people won't follow through. The one constant is always your bigger picture.

Stay aligned with your end goal but as change happens, see where it leads. Instead of having your mind set, have a mindset of opportunity. Trends, interests and consumer buying habits shift often. The success you saw last year can quickly take a turn without constant feedback and change. Netflix is a great example of this. Since launching in 1997 as a DVD mail-based company they have continued to evolve into the world's largest subscription streaming service. Imagine if they didn't embrace consumer viewing habits. Change is good, enjoy the process.

## KNOW YOU'RE THE EXPERT

Imposter syndrome as an entrepreneur is real. I've seen some of the most talented people I know start to question their expertise when transitioning into entrepreneurship. You no longer have someone providing constant feedback, annual reviews, or raises to validate success. Now your self-worth is up to you. Never forget, you are the expert in your chosen field or business. At some point your passion and expertise led you to be an entrepreneur. That was not by mistake. You earned the place you are now, and you are an expert at what you do.

Find ways to celebrate your own success. Cheers a glass of champagne to yourself when you have a big win. Invite friends over for dinner to celebrate a profitable quarter. Bring yourself on vacation to unwind after a big launch. You have to be your biggest advocate. I stated this earlier but being an entrepreneur can be lonely. You have to give yourself permission to celebrate you. Remember why you started. You don't think you're the best, you know.

## IN CONCLUSION

As entrepreneurs, our mindset can be our biggest obstacle. Change the way you think and watch the opportunities come your way. Believe that you are destined for success and break down the limiting beliefs that are stopping you from getting there. If you want something, it is already yours. You just have to make the decision to go after it. Each of us was created with a unique gift, what is yours? You've got this.

***

To Contact Kate:

Kate@KateRaeDigital.com or find her on social media at @KateRaeDigital.

# Vishal Bajpai

Vishal Bajpai is an entrepreneur of an automotive cyber security company. He is a co-founder and CEO of SecureThings. He has over 20 years of extensive experience as a visionary leader, motivator, technology and product strategist for the emerging markets. His mission is to safeguard this society from the cyber threats, especially in the automotive eco-system. His core wiring is that of a profound innovator. He is passionate about autonomous & connected vehicles cyber security emerging market, evangelizing and building innovative solutions to solve real customer problems. He keeps presenting his thought leadership on cyber security challenges in the changing automotive value chain in different forums.

Before starting his own venture, Vishal worked with some of industry leading organization like Symantec and provided his thought leadership to many industry leading enterprise products. He was involved in many innovation forums and contributed protecting organization's IP. Vishal has a master's degree in computers and stay in the bay area.

# Dream Big

## Faith and passion will turn it into reality

***By Vishal Bajpai***

**Small Beginnings.**

I have always been a techie at heart. As I think back, I feel that in many curious ways my life has been designed around technology. At first my alma mater was at the core of my existence, then came another techie -*My wife.* And now technology in the automotive cyber security industry has become my driving force. I am bowled over by innovation.

Like magic that binds together a story in a fiction book, technology has linked together many of the crucial experiences in my life. I met my soulmate during my time in college, and we bonded over an interesting computers network problem that we were trying to solve at IIT Kanpur, India during our internship. I have to confess though; along with her I was getting attracted to another idea that was slowly building up in my mind. That day, while solving that problem, I made another promise to myself. I was going to start my own technological venture in Silicon Valley. While it was a long shot then and seemed improbable in every way, but I sowed the seed of ambition securely deep within and nurtured it with care over the coming years. "Difficult but not impossible", I kept on telling myself.

Cut two –years later life put my wife and me together as professional colleagues in a leading Cyber Security organization. At work, we were like soldiers on a digital battlefield. During the formative years of our career we would often be appalled by the damage a malware could do and would discuss at length about the tactical solutions that could help society avert these threats and feel safe to embrace these technologies. Every day used to be a new challenge exposing us to new customer problems. But, the quest for starting our own venture never died. This experience helped establish a strong foundation on which I would build my future dream – my own enterprise.

Now that I look back, I realize – these tactical conversations and the passion for cyber security propelled me to start my own venture in the automotive cyber security.

**Shooting Ducks.**

With experience, in both winning and failing, I have chalked out the time for disruption much like the sport of shooting ducks. Timing is very important here. You wait patiently, estimate the speed, distance and right time for the duck to be in target, and only then you take your shot.

I had been waiting for a crucial problem that we could solve. Whether it was coffee with our techie friends, or back home, we always spoke about "What-Could-Be" in the face of technology. Simultaneously we were working in the most happening of fields. IoT, Machine Learning and cutting-edge technologies that were going to re-imagine our lives on earth. The eco-system was constantly changing. Tesla was creating disruptions, new business models were shaping up, ride share taxies were not a dream anymore, and every business model seemed to connect one more aspect of our life to the internet. Whether it was our house, our cars, our phones – all these important aspects around which our lives revolved were getting connected intrinsically with each other.

Identifying the exact problem to solve coupled with a deep understanding of its impact is the right direction to take. This helped me firm up my future course.

All the technological transformation sounded brilliant. But every coin has another side. Our more than 15 years in the industry pushed us to think of all those who would exploit these evolutions thus giving a view of the stiff competition that we are likely to face. Cyber threats have evolved since the late 1980s when they were first recorded. With the world around transforming into a Digital first society - cyber threats cast a very dark shadow on each of these meaningful evolutions. Transportation is evolving from personal to multimodal, shared and autonomous, the dangers of cyber-attacks therefore cannot be highlighted enough. Having spent more than a decade in the cyber-security domain, we were fully aware of its criticality. Most of the population, uses some sort of transportation in day to day life. The devastating impact of cyber-attacks on the transport system could destroy our confidence.

Our big opportunity came as we both were tasked to look at automotive cybersecurity domain while working in the R&D division our organization.

**Taking a Leap:**

You need to be fearless to become a leader. Embrace the challenge and shine.

Jumping from the computers industry to the automotive industry was a big step and lot of things were at stake as we assumed this new responsibility. But like every great risk, the stakes were high, and so were the rewards. We worked extensively with a couple of BIG automotive manufacturers and universities which helped us understand the intricacies of automobiles, its architecture and were surprised to know that a vehicle is like a network of small computers called microcontrollers. The entire experience of vehicle manufacturing was new – but exciting. Like any student, we absorbed everything we could and entered into the ethical hacking world by exploiting vulnerabilities to control a vehicle, this was all in a controlled environment and for learning the system better.

**A fork in the road:**

Sometimes you need to follow your instinct, have faith in your expertise and take a tough decision. One always gets opportunities in life to do something big but recognizing them and grabbing them at that instant is the crucial decision where the weak fail.

Entrepreneurial success is never a rising vertical line. It is a series of ongoing waves, with its highs and lows but there is always light at the end of the tunnel. One just has to be at it.

We set up our organization with as much care and thought as we could. We had an awareness all through that big business comes with its own set of risks. The time I was working with the previous organization, the market was not completely ready for automotive cyber security products and hence there came a sudden change in the ecosystem. Unfortunately (now fortunately) I stood my ground and did not blindly join the herd. I was convinced deep within that the need for the technology on the domain I was researching was definitely going to resurface. I had two options – find a whole new space to work in or go with my belief.

It was then, that I decided to leave my lucrative job and pursue the dream I always had. The contribution that I could make to the society through this new venture made me more committed to take on this challenge as an entrepreneur.

**Strong Support System:**

When you plan to go into an unknown territory, you need to have a strong support system that always gives you strength. There are times when you feel that you are drained, and you need energy from your close pals.

Cars need wheels to keep moving, technology needs power to keep going, and people need support to keep growing. I see that in my wife and 12-year-old son. They are my inspiration and strength. I discussed my decision with my family, and they gave rock-solid support and stood by my decision. It was a joint dream of my wife and me, but our strategy was that one would take the risk while the other would continue working to keep the wheels of the family well-oiled. I did sacrifice spending enough quality time with my son, but I guess he understands my compulsions.

**Clarity and Numbers – Can do wonders!**

What is most required is a clear vision on what you plan to do. It must be backed up by thorough research on the problem statement, target geography and the target market to avoid any major surprises. Your business plan cannot be the same always. Just like your market, your plan needs to be flexible and you need to be prepared for all constant change in the variables that matter. Deep knowledge of the industry is non-negotiable here. Everything else gets build around it.

I was fortunate enough to have worked extensively in the target domain for more than a couple of years before starting my own venture. I had to now identify the solution that can hit the exact problem. I also got help from a couple of extremely knowledgeable people to validate my strategies early on and refine them. The result of this effort is indeed rewarding. Despite passing different phases of our venture and the customers validation our enterprise continues to revolve largely around the initial Big Idea. Yes, some strategical changes are obvious considering the competitions and change in the market dynamics.

One of the critical aspects of the business development and sales is talking to the customer in his/her own vocabulary, so it is extremely important to study and start using a language that your target industry understands.

**Lean Mean Tech Machine:**

Like I mentioned, a strong and clear vision, attracts strong and reliable minds. As you go along, you will find guys who believe in your story and can be a great value add. You need to keep your eyes open to look and pick the right team.

I am fortunate enough to have a team that I am proud of. Conversations that started over a mere cup of coffee, have turned into bonds that have made technological leaps. I identified the perfect mix of experience and a healthy curiosity of youth that gives you a perfect blend of success. My team members are the real stars of the show.

**Failing is a good thing:**

Starting your venture is bound to bring you a bunch of setbacks. You can't change this result, but you can change your response to this result. Your perseverance and resolve can convert a market from failing to see the problem into actively needing a solution. It is your passion that drives you in testing times. Passion is energy that dictates the success as well as gives you enough ammunition when it is required to fight against survival. You need to draw self-motivation and that energy gives power to the folks around you. Your passion and energy also help in binding the team together in the difficult periods.

We were targeting a new market and I admit first year was a bit tough. But we were able to tweak our sales and marketing strategy enough to convince our customers in our vision.

Often entrepreneurs don't realize that failures are a good thing. Each failure brings you a lesson, and a parameter to better your product, and transform it into a seamless solution. Consider your local parameters and modify your messaging to help your customer understand your vision. Your idea may be years ahead of the market, but if you can conquer the "WHY" behind your idea first, and then move on to the "WHAT" no one can stop your audience from coming to you.

Always set your eyes on the emerging opportunities and technological evolutions while demonstrating the ability to make changes accordingly.

While working on a certain geography, we were quick to chance upon the government's push for electric vehicles and were quick to see how many of the manufacturers began revamping their strategies. This opened up an entirely new market to us that we initially didn't think of *-protecting the electric vehicle and the charging infrastructure from cyber threats.*

**Financial Planning:**

There is this unreasonable dream that most start-ups have regarding funding. We believe that we will get funded almost instantly and the rest of the ride is going to be smooth. But reality works very differently. You need to have better financial planning to cover up your expenses so that they don't dry up at the time of need. A good financial backing also keeps you protected from financial crunch situations. You don't want to accept terms that may result in you executing your plans against your better judgement. There is another aspect of financial planning. You have to be extremely aware of where you are investing and ensure that it is aligned to your priority. To share one example, there was a company doing well and they conducted a comprehensive campaign to raise funds in a double digit of millions of dollars. Once the funding was done, they changed the strategy, put up a big team just to see that there are very few takers on the new idea and the business model. But by that time, they had exhausted a majority of their funds.

**Open to new alliances:**

As we grew, we quickly realized that the customer looks for an effective solution that can solve their specific needs. Each customer may have different complexities and challenges. Also, they look at the system as a whole and it is not possible for a single organization to solve all their issues.

Finding the right partners on the way and working in tandem is the wise thing to do. Fail fast and rectify even faster - this is a proven way to be agile and ready to hit the nail on its head. It is required to create a trusted ecosystem for other innovative partners to come and join your initiative if you want to solve the challenges the world is going to face.

**Stay hungry. Stay foolish.**

There is no alternative to knowledge. The more you learn, the more you will come to know that there is plenty more to learn. Knowledge opens a door in your mind to look at things differently and be innovative. Learn how to be disruptive. You need to be disruptive to sustain and keep growing in the market.

Here is a method that I follow for generating innovative ideas. A long time back, while having a causal chat with my wife, she shared a beautiful thought taking the analogy of a seed. Take a seed and nurture it into a big plant that can give fruits, shelter and inspiration to others. This was an amazing thing. Another method I follow is to come up with a crazy idea and then correlate that into the domain and some of existing or potential future problems that you envision the customer may hit. This, I found, is a great way of generating disruptive ideas. First time I shared these thoughts in an innovation summit we had with the higher management and stakeholders, and this was a big hit. It is the methodology of my life to look at things differently and constantly innovating. The same is the success mantra of my current venture. We look at the problems differently and come up with disruptive thoughts.

When your motivation is to make a positive contribution to the larger world, it is bound to be a customer delight. You also need to have good set of advisors with diverse skill sets that can fill your skill gap as well as positively challenge you in different decisions you take to extract the best.

**Testimonials and a Testament to Yourself**

Continuous assessment is a must to ensure that you are on the right trajectory. This requires extra focus, but it is worth it when you see smiles on faces of people associated with you. Who can be a better judge than your customers, investors and the team you are closely working with?

Today, I see the world's top manufacturers looking at us to protect their vehicles from cyber threats by using our protection solutions. We are being consulted by the world's leading and innovative automotive manufacturers to help build a strong and secure design, or top suppliers look at us to secure their entire ecosystem. As a bonus - A world renowned business consulting firm recognized our efforts by nominating us for their top leadership award. It is a testimony of the leader we became in this industry reaffirming the progress we are making. It is a delight for our customers, our investors and our stakeholders as well as my team who continuously burn the midnight oil to produce something unique and compelling.

Now, when I look back at this fascinating journey *(that still has some miles on it)*, the belief gets stronger that it is a MUST to dream to achieve something big. It must be complimented by clear vision, your passion, commitment and perseverance. There is never an end, the journey must go on, bars must be raised, new goals must be set always, new paths must be redrawn!

When you look back - you will always think you could have done better. But that is a testament to the fact that you are constantly growing. Keep dreaming and help others dream, be fearless and be an adventurer.

***

To contact Vishal:

Linked-in: http://www.linkedin.com/in/bajpaivishal

Twitter: @ivishalbajpai

Email: bajpai.vishal@yahoo.com

## Terry Perez

Terry Perez is a Passionate and Hardworking executive and marketing professional. She has over 30 years 'experience in the Direct Sales industry. Skilled in talent recruiting and customer relations. Outstanding in presentation, communication and cross-cultural team management skills. High-energy, results-oriented leader with an entrepreneurial attitude.

Terry has launched well-received professional development courses, training courses and success workbooks for many network marketing companies. She has mentored and coached distributors resulting in 15% and more growth in productivity. Former owner and Licensed Administrator of the Seven Oaks Assisted Living Center, where she managed every facet of the business.

She has built teams as high as 100 thousand distributors in three direct sales companies that all produced substantial residual incomes on a monthly basis. Her Organizations have been the springboards for many industry leaders who have went on to become top builders and producers. Terry has earned top recruiter, sales and President's Club awards in three major direct sales companies.

She founded W.O.W. (Women of Wonder) in 2009 to present. She has written three books "Dream Big I Dare Me," "Dare to Be Great," and "The Diet Solution."

## Dream Big I DARE ME

### *By Terry Perez*

Every Challenge brings a positive outcome ~ Ruby Ewing

Along my own journey with success, I am often surprised by the enlightenment that I receive in merely reminding myself of the power of ASKING for what I want. It seems simple, but it can be a crucial piece in getting what you want; in your life, your business, and in your relationships. Ironically, it is often left out of the success formula!

Statistics report that over 60% of the time, a salesperson doesn't ASK for the sale! Can you believe that? All that time spent presenting and courting the prospect, and yet, leaving out the critical ingredient– ASKING for the purchase or the business! That's like hosting Thanksgiving dinner and forgetting the turkey. You've got to ask!

Asking is, in my opinion, the world's most influential and neglected secret to success and happiness. So why don't we ask? If it's that easy, what holds us back? The answer is the same for every roadblock of our success: FEAR!! Fear that we will get a no to the request, although ironically, we get a no anyways by not asking.

We are afraid that we might look dumb or needy or desperate or so "uncool" by making a request. We simply do not want to approach our partner, a friend, our boss, a prospect, a potential date with what we need. People make more decisions from fear than faith. If we don't ask, we have no way to get the thing we want…Know that you are worthy of your dreams! Make them decisively bold! It is essential to THINK BIG when it comes to goals for your future. The key to dreaming big is to accept and appreciate the abundant life that the Universe has to offer you. You have a right to live fully and freely.

I recommend you think big thoughts, dream big dreams, and make big plans. Say to yourself positive affirmations like "Good now flows into my life from expected and unexpected channels." "I am always presented with new and wonderful opportunities." A person who cannot conceive of anything beyond what they can see with their natural eyes misses out on the best God has planned for them. A hope, vision, dream, or plan is like a seed. We cannot have a harvest without a seed, and it's the same way with our desires.

The biggest mistake a person can make is to have no dreams for the FUTURE and do nothing to make anything in their life better. The famous Colonial Sanders of KFC – Kentucky Fried Chicken, was in his 60's when someone finally said YES to his chicken recipe and began the great franchise of KFC. He had a big dream and believed in the power of his vision. Do you know how many times he was told "no" to his request, to his idea, to his DREAM? Over 1,000 times!! Now that's persistence! He certainly believed in *his* dream.

I learned this valuable lesson over 30 years ago. I had a big dream to run and to own an Assisted Living Facility. My vision was of a home where older adults could live in a peaceful, caring, vibrant community. The residents could spend time doing the things they enjoyed. In my imagination, it needed to be small enough to feel like a big family home. I had been dreaming of this since I worked for my Aunt Veda at her Assisted Living Facility in Maryland when I was 16.

Years later, out of the blue, I was driving on a country road in North Carolina, totally lost. As I was turning around, my eye caught an abandoned School building. Back in the early 80's, we had no cell phones or GPS, and I got lost quite a bit. I will never forget turning the corner and seeing this beautiful brick schoolhouse with a majestic mountain positioned perfectly behind it. I immediately saw the potential of it becoming an Assisted Living Facility.

I had no idea on how to contact the person who owned it, nor how I would get the money to buy it. I believed in my dream. I have lovely parents who instilled in me that nothing is impossible; the very word says *I'm Possible.* For weeks I would drive by the property, peek inside the windows and walk the grounds. I would take my children and let them play on the grounds, all the while imagining myself owning this property and living there.

I would say these words: "This property is mine by Divine right; I claim it in the name above all names… Thank you!" No one taught me this; it just came to me one day to say, so I just started saying it. Every week I would drive to Nebo and began to see new things there… benches for residents to sit on, beautiful flowers, a garden, even the name 7 Oaks (7 oak trees were framing the property). There was a house close by, and I thought to myself, I could live here and run the place. I was young and had very little money, but I had a big dream and when you dream big dreams…magic happens!

My husband and I had just moved from Florida and had my daughter, who was barely 3 weeks old, and my son David who was 3. We were temporarily living with my parents in their basement apartment. Every day I would share my dream and vision, and then I decided to ASK… ask my parents if they would go on this success journey and partner up. Daddy said if I found out who owned it and we could get financing as well as half the down payment for the loan, he would go along. I think my Dad really didn't believe we could pull it off. However, *I* saw this so clearly in my mind and had faith that somehow, it would be my reality.

After a few weeks of driving to the property, I saw a man cutting branches from the apple trees that lined the edge of the property. I decided to ask if he might know who owned the schoolhouse. He knew so many wonderful details about the school and that the county owned the school and 5 acres, and that it was to be auctioned in 2 weeks. I raced back to Ashville, and by now, my Mother and Dad were convinced we should go for this big dream of mine.

We got all the details for what to do, and the last step was getting a bank to say yes. My Mother and I went to 4 banks, who all said no. These were banks where both Grandfather and my parents had an account! We just didn't know any more banks to go to accept my bank. It didn't cross my mind to go to my bank as I only had around $100 in there. As we were leaving the last bank, my Mother turned around and asked the loan officer if she could give us a referral of a bank that would consider backing us. She told us that we should go to NCNB and that Ed Gent would be a possibility as he actually went to the school and had a fondness for the property. WOW! I looked at my Mother and said… That's my bank!

I made an assumption that because my Mother had no account there, this bank wouldn't qualify me for the loan. As it turned out, she was right, and we got the building and turned it into 7 Oaks Assisted Living. Ed Gent also gave us the information to get the building and what to ask in the Bid. He told My Mother to put a bid in at $80,000. My Daddy said that was great, but Terry Lynn how are you going to come up with the 10% down? I told my Daddy there were miracles when you believe with all your heart and soul… I reminded him of his words: *You can have anything you desire if you believe.* Daddy was a Networker in Shaklee and He looked at me and said, "ok let's see how the Universe responds to your dream."

My husband and everyone around me said I had lost my mind, and there was no way I could come up with $8,500 in less than 5 days to put in the private Bid. I prayed every day and thanked God for sending me the $8,500. On the 3rd day, I went to the mailbox, and I received a letter from my uncle Jeff. The letter stated that My grandpa Herbert who died, wanted me to have his silver dollar collection (It was a toe sack full of silver dollars)! I cashed in the silver dollars, and it was over $9,000! We serve a big God, and he has big plans for us all. We got the Bid for pennies on the dollar, all because we ASKED for it and believed!

I believe the reason I got my dream was I had the right vibration…I felt it as real. You have to FEEL the joy, happiness, love that comes from having that thing you desire. When you are holding the feeling of that frequency, the Universe lines up. We are all energy, and everything on this earth vibrates at a certain frequency.

Think of it this way. Just like a radio channel, we are looking for the right station to listen to. When you find the song you like, you stop and stay for a while. When you hold the whole picture in your mind, you begin to send out that vibration, and that frequency goes out like a strong signal and begins to bring back what you desire.

It is because of my journey for these few decades that I am convinced; we are capable of getting anything we truly desire. Everything that is possible is seeking expression through us. God wants those who can play music to have pianos and every other instrument, and to have the means to cultivate their talents to the fullest extent… "IT is God that worketh in you to will and to do," said Paul. Don't hesitate in ASKING largely; "it is your Father's pleasure to give you the kingdom," said Jesus.

This experience taught me to take the leap of faith even if I can't see what's under me. I am reminded of the movie with Harrison Ford in

Indiana Jones, where he is standing on the other side of getting the Holy Grail. He can't see what's between him and the other side but clouds. When he throws rocks in the air, he hears them land on something solid. That was enough for him to take the leap of faith and get to the other side.

Since this experience, my faith is unshakable. Asking for what you want is the key to getting what you want. Actively pursuing your big dream is the other key, and thirdly, you must FEEL it to be real. You must ACT and not be passive. Are you doing your part, or just sitting around with a bad attitude waiting for someone else to fix your life?

God wants to motivate you from the inside. He gives creative ideas, big dreams, and an aggressive, creative attitude. He allows you to miss your plane or to get lost and to still find your path. Declare out loud; you will not just sit in the middle of a mess or situation and waste your life. Declare you will say YES to an active, aggressive, creative person who dreams big, and you refuse to give up. So, make peace in your mind when you're told no, it doesn't need to be taken personally, you're no worse off – you're actually the same, and someone somewhere will say YES. Every Challenge brings a positive outcome, and change has an opportunity inside it. I have experienced this many times in my life. No matter how bad it may seem, I always look for the positive.

My Daddy used to tell the story of how I wanted a pony so bad I drew pictures of my pony and talked about my pony constantly. One-day Daddy took me to a neighbor's barn, and it was full of manure. I got so excited and started yelling, "Daddy, Daddy, thank you"! I knew I would get it!! My Daddy was bewildered at this reaction, and he asked me why I was so excited to see a big pile of manure…Because Daddy, there must be a pony in there somewhere. Needless to say, I got a pony 2 weeks later. Sometimes we will "miss the plane" How you respond is the key.

Always keep in mind that your mess is the message, and the challenge is the gift. There is a gold mine of potential hidden in each one of us, and you are no exception. This great potential is directly connected to our dreams and visions. God plants them in our heart or spirit, as a seed in the form of a thought or desire. Over time the seed grows as we feed it. When you move in the direction of your dreams, you will meet it in an odd hour just like I did and so many before me. Every day I spend a few minutes and walk around my house, hotel, wherever I am, and I look at what I appreciate. I want you to get in the habit of appreciation and Dream Big I dare you!

*"All our dreams can come true if we dare to pursue them."*

*~WALT DISNEY~*

**My Top 5 DARES**

Think about how great God is and then remind yourself He is on your side

Make a list of your dreams, and don't limit yourself to a certain number. Keep adding to the list as ideas come to you. You will be amazed at how many of them will indeed come true. (I create a vision board every year) Keep a Success Journal and write in it every day.

Make a plan to pursue at least one of your dreams. Ask yourself what it will take to succeed: Money? Work ethic? More education? A Team of people? Once you have a good idea, work hard to make it happen.

Dream BIG. But celebrate the small steps of success along the way. Realize that each effort you make is one step closer to the discipline and dedication required to focus your passion to what's calling you. Keep your love large and in charge of your dreams. Give it your all and refuse to give up.

Give back to someone every day. It can be a phone call, a note, buying someone's meal. Whatever that looks like for you.

*"Continuous **effort**~ not strength or intelligence~*

*is the key to unlocking our **potential**."*

*~Winston Churchhill~*

***

To Contact Terry:

1-281-883-8816

Dreambig360@gmail.com

www.thediamondmaker.com

## Matthew Hardy

A Self-proclaimed Renaissance man, MJ Hardy is a Veteran with over 22 years of service, a leader for a Fortune 500 consulting firm, a successful published author, transformational subject matter expert, community activist, and entrepreneur. MJ Hardy has a passion for helping veterans and their families plant their feet on solid ground as they transition into civilian life. For those outside of the military, MJ wants to assist the "everyday' person exit off the superhighway of mediocrity and achieve their goals and objectives. As a leader, he cares about you! He appreciates the challenges and difficulties you are facing as you begin your transformation. As a coach, he will assist you in the development of the skills that you need to transition successfully. As a mentor, he will advise and provide you with the tools that you need. He believes that he establishes a vital ongoing relationship with you that is based upon mutual respect, trust, open and honest communications. His vision is to assist forgotten service members as they transition from their isolated military life and help them create a bridge to their civilian life and communities as smooth and meaningful as possible. For the "everyday' person to bring new meaning to their lives.

## Every Man

### *By Matthew (MJ) Hardy*

> *"We mostly spend [our] lives conjugating three verbs: to Want, to Have, and to Do... forgetting that none of these verbs have any ultimate significance, except so far as they are transcended by and included in, the fundamental verb, to Be." Evelyn Underhill*

Aloha and Shalom, my sisters and brothers.

I am not giving you the keys to unlock the doors to great wealth. I am not providing you with a secret handshake, tricks for manipulating Amazon's algorithms, or tips to write compelling Facebook advertisements. I understand you may be searching for that 'silver bullet' or 'magic formula' or single key that will open the door to all that you desire. I get it.

In the short time that we have together, I ask for your indulgence, patience, and an open mind. I believe there is value in a more holistic approach to a better you—a more complete you. I will share with you some personal anecdotes; although seemingly ordinary, they help to drive home some teaching points.

**Selfless Service**

Look no further. Look in a mirror and 'see' the answer—the answer is within you. When you understand and appreciate who you are, and that takes primacy over all other plans and pleasures in your life. When you are not indebted by money, because you have a definite purpose. When you realize your life's mission. Why you were placed on this Earth, then you've already come a long way to obtaining inner peace. By helping others, you will begin to take action that is based upon your uniqueness that incorporates your strengths, skills, talents, and desires to be the best possible you.

We are living in an instant gratification and "*what's in it for me?*" driven society. We value notoriety and affluence over good works. I believe that is, in part, a reason so many of us today are miserable. We are chasing an elusive dream that has little value. We drink, smoke, and indulge our way to numbness to avoid feeling emotions.

We enjoy watching a person reach the highest levels of fame and then take morbid pleasure in watching them fall. We have become the modern-day personification of the seven deadly sins: Pride, Envy, Gluttony, Lust, Anger, Greed, and Sloth, but there is hope.

For all our superficiality, we still admire individuals that exemplify the 'greatness of soul.' We look to Abraham Lincoln, Mahatma Gandhi, Dr. Martin Luther King, Jr., Nelson Mandela, and Mother Teresa, as some examples. Despite their differences, they all shared a universal value of helping others. They are the epitome of selflessness and personal courage. Unlike celebrities, their legacies still live on today.

Let us look at Jesus Christ. His ministry was about three years, he walked wherever he went, and he drew large crowds. There were no cell phones, Amazon, or Facebook. Yet, a carpenter's son, a man of modest means, and with his twelve disciples created and grew one of the most well-known faiths in the world that still exists over two thousand years later. When threatened by the Romans and other religious leaders at that time, he could have acquiesced, but he was absolute in his beliefs. Regardless of the concerns, Jesus believed in his message. People flocked to him because they hungered for his simple message of love, hope, and forgiveness.

Nelson Mandela said, "What counts in life is not the mere fact that we have lived. It is what difference we have made to the lives of others that will determine the significance of the life we lead." He demonstrated personal courage and resolve to stand up to others for others' equal rights, education, and a better life. Despite being locked away in a terrible prison and inhumanely treated, Nelson Mandela never gave up. His legacy of hope, forgiveness, and healing stands as a beacon to the rest of the world.

When I was growing up, all I ever wanted to be was either a Soldier, policeman, or priest. I wanted to make a positive and lasting difference in those around me. In some small way through my talents, time, selflessness, and generosity that I could make someone smile, help them through a difficult time, see the value in themselves, or achieve their life's goals. For me, I didn't want to sleepwalk through my day, my week, my year, and my life oblivious to what is going on around me. I want all my endeavors to have meaning.

For example, I've supported numerous charities not only financially, but with time and talents. I've volunteered at soup kitchens, ran miles for one, and walked miles for another. I've done landscaping and painted homes for disabled Veterans and the elderly. I've read to classes. Through Junior Achievement, I've taught financial literacy to elementary school students. At every opportunity, I was willing to support whenever and wherever I could.

After I retired from the Army, I wanted to become involved in the community, so I signed up to be a Big Brother. When I told my family about my actions, my three children looked at me and said, "aren't we enough." When I proceeded to tell them how this teenager was in foster care and had been in and out of juvenile delinquent homes, they said, you are the right man for him.

Over the next four years, my 'little' and I both learned a lot about ourselves, the law, and how society treats those from more marginalized backgrounds. There were times when I would have to travel a long way to visit him in a juvenile detention center or take time off work to observe court hearings. Trying to connect with a thirteen-year-old troubled youth and show him the right way wasn't always fun. They were some tough and challenging times. I sometimes wondered if all this work was worth it; however, I didn't cave into my short-sightedness and let my frustrations stop me.

First and foremost, I've grown as a person, because I embraced the hardships and the challenges because I knew that I'd be a better man for working through them. My armor is not bright and polished. My armor has dents, nicks, and worn from all of life's battles, but I know that my armor will serve me well because it has been tested and will weather any challenge that I may decide to take on in the future. Second, I've met some incredible and thoughtful people that made a real difference in peoples' lives for absolutely no money or recognition. In the end, all the positives have far outweighed any short-term discomforts.

I chose to serve. Today, I continue to make that simple decision because by creating value in others' lives, then I have created value in my own life, too. Never in my mind did I believe that I would have achieved, see, and experienced what I have for almost fifty years. I've never gone hungry. I've always had enough money to take care of my family, friends, community, and myself. I've never wanted.

Write your obituary. What would you write? If you asked others to write it for you, what would they write? Try it. I'm not asking for you to regurgitate a laundry list of accomplishments, but to think deeply and thoughtfully about who you are. What have you written? What have others written about you? Granted, a simple exercise, but I want to challenge you to become a better person—I want you to be proud of yourself. You will be happier and more fulfilled by serving others selflessly.

**Relationships**

The company that one keeps does matter and reflects on the type of person that you are. I'm a Caucasian man and a product of Irish American family values raised in a middle-class suburb of Detroit. My two best friends are Jim and Carl. My white, middle-class upbringing could not have been more different than the childhood experiences of both Jim and Carl. Jim, an African American, grew up in a major city with a limited socio-economic background. He once recounted the trauma of his cousin shot in the back of the head over a drug deal went bad. Carl grew up in Puerto Rico, where he experienced abandonment and abuse by family members.

Jim and Carl could have let their life experiences predicate the type of men that they would become; however, Jim and Carl were determined to have better lives. They have had successful military careers, continue to work successfully in other industries, and are both comfortably middle class. When you look at where both men came from, what they had to overcome, and all they've accomplished—their successes have surpassed many with much larger bank accounts and more considerable notoriety. I've learned more from them than any millionaire that I know. They are not perfect men, but men of character. I hold them as examples of determination and not accepting the status quo.

Although geographically separated, we always reach out to each other. We seem to have a sixth sense and know when someone is in need, and chances are we have already contacted each other. Although our life experiences and histories are dramatically different, my friendship with these men is cemented in mutual respect. I find comfort knowing in my heart-of-hearts that these men would lay their lives down for me just as I would for them. I could not ask for better friends.

I'm also not referring to the number of followers that you may have on your Twitter, Instagram, or Facebook accounts either. I don't care. I find it humorous when someone will post on their Facebook page, "I'm sorry, I can't accept any more friendships, because Facebook won't allow me to have over 5,000." Have they gotten to the point that their validation as a person is by the number of 'Friends'? Then, they're surprised and hurt when the 'trolls' go after them. More importantly, when they need a friend, they have a difficult time finding one.

I'm not interested in the quantity, but the quality of my relationships. I want relationships in my life that genuinely care for me and want to see me succeed in life; however. I also have an obligation to care and want others to succeed genuinely. I need to take time to care and nurture these relationships. Like selfless service, I have an increased sense of belonging and purpose. I receive other benefits, such as an increase in happiness, reduce stress, and talk through life's challenges.

Thirty-eight years ago, Heather and I became friends when we met in college. Over the years, we've always found time to check on each other regardless of being separated by thousands of miles, times zones, and oceans. Like Jim and Carl, Heather's friendship is important to me because she is an excellent sounding board and a significant moral compass.

One day, Heather reached out to me and sent me a note. She wrote that she felt her life had hit a plateau where she just seemed to be moving sideways. She was existing. I wrote back, "what are you talking about? First, you have a husband who, after thirty-eight years of marriage, still loves you wildly and adores you. Next, you have three incredibly well adjusted and successful children. Finally, you're an incredible educator who has had a tremendous positive impact on students' lives that will last forever. You've achieved so much. You made it!" She wrote back, "thank you. Your words are just what I needed to hear."

Heather and I have a mutual friend, Martha. Martha is a wonderful woman who never has anything wrong to say about anyone. She doesn't have a mean bone in her body. Martha always has everyone's best interests at heart. Martha is a joy to be around, and I marvel at the sunshine she radiates. She is a true blessing.

I noticed that Martha was posting less on Facebook, and when she did post, they were characteristically unlike her. I reached out to Heather and told her my concerns that I thought that something might be wrong with Martha. Heather found out that Martha was having severe health issues. Heather and I began to call Martha regularly to provide her with words of encouragement and support. Fortunately, Martha was able to overcome her health issues.

I would encourage you to start making a more considerable effort in your relationships, especially for those that matter. I'm not looking for adulation. I value relationships that are more deep and sincere. As I've grown older, these relationships make me feel better and have a more significant impact on my well-being. The well-known eighty-year-old Harvard study documents this point; "Close relationships, more than money or fame, are what keep people happy throughout their lives, . . . Those ties protect people from life's discontents, help to delay mental and physical decline, and are better predictors of long and happy lives than social class, IQ, or even genes[1]."

## Spirituality

How do you tap into your spiritual side? How do you experience a power greater than one's self? Although, I'm not talking about religiosity. For Christians, believing that Christ resides within themselves and through prayer and meditation, they can receive the answers, strength, and guidance they seek. For Nichiren Buddhists, their simple mantra of "Namu Myoho Renge Kyo" taps into the universal energy within themselves to stop suffering and start living. Mysticism believes that a connection can be made with God through

---

[1] Mineo, Liz, Good Genes are Nice, but Joy is Better, Harvard Gazette, April 11, 2017, internet, December 27, 2019.

prayer and meditation. Whatever means you choose; I would highly encourage you to find your spirituality and to tap into this energy.

Discard the phones, watches, and every other piece of technology and go to a quiet and comforting place. Learn to embrace the silence and listen for the calm and encouraging voice that speaks within you. Don't be discouraged by your mental distraction as thoughts and memories as they come flooding in. They will arise during your period of reflection. Please give them away to the universal energy. Allow yourself to ponder and invite internal dialogue. Do not expect the ground to move beneath your feet or filled with rapture. The universal energy does not reach out and shake us, but tenderly invites us ever more thoughtfully in its presence.

Every morning, my wife and I silently meditate for thirty minutes. We enjoy moments of silence to contemplate what is essential in our lives and what are our next steps. I've learned to listen, appreciate, and draw upon the surrounding energy. I've learned to be a child again; I wonder at rainbows and cloud formations. I enjoy taking a walk-in nature.

On my walks, I'll take pictures of beautiful flowers that I see and post them on my Facebook page. People marvel at their beauty and ask, "where did you take these?" I smile because I'll find the flowers sometimes in the most surprising places. I've been in neighborhoods where cars are parked on cinder blocks and "beware of dogs" hang from the chain-linked fence. I give thanks to

the beauty wherever I travel. It's all around us. These walks are a form of meditation and help me appreciate all that I have in my life.

My spirituality brings balance and reason in my life. It has improved troubled relationships—it saved my marriage. Additionally, I find answers to my most pressing questions and concerns. However, I've also learned not to have 'specific' expectations of those answers. Most often, the answers will come from the least expected places, when I least expect it, and much better than I ever could have imagined.

I greatly appreciate your patience and an open mind. I realize that the depth and breadth of this subject are wide-ranging and vast. I could have covered other material, but I've chosen to only write about three specific areas because I thought they were the ones that mattered most from an interpersonal and intrapersonal perspective. Hold yourself accountable and make every detail of everyday life more meaningful by caring for others. The answer is you!

Aloha and Shalom,

***

To contact Matthew:

info@alphacivilian.com

https://www.alphacivilian.com/

https://www.facebook.com/Coach-MJ-Hardy-368020797137803/?modal=admin_todo_tour

https://www.linkedin.com/in/matthew-hardy-885211101/

https://www.amazon.com/MJ-Hardy/e/B014ZGM64M?ref_=dbs_p_pbk_r00_abau_000000

https://www.facebook.com/readmjhardy/?modal=admin_todo_tour

https://readmjhardy.weebly.com/

# Evans Duren

Evans Duren is a Motivational Christian Speaker, inspiring audiences to shatter the lines between business and faith!

Named by Talent Concierge as one of its top three best platform speakers on personal development, he is a natural storyteller who combines his faith with a passion for business and personal empowerment, equipping audiences to live their lives fully alive.

Recognized as a dominant force as a top sales producer in the Fortune 15 and Tech Start-up spaces, he brings fresh wisdom that can only come from years of practicing his craft while building genuine relationships that last well beyond a transaction.

Through the victories, losses, struggles, and triumphs inside and outside the walls of business, today's top business leaders rely on Evans to walk beside them as they work through his blockbuster self-help program to rEDefine Success in their business and personal life.

Evans believes each of us is a uniquely and divinely created individual with an incredible opportunity to grow and impact the world through our businesses by fully leveraging our gifts, skills, and talents. Anyone can be ordinary; Evans will dare you to be extraordinary!

He resides in South Carolina with his wife, Jamye, and two sons, Clark and Wyatt. When he is not writing, coaching, or speaking, Evans spends time with his family and enjoys the outdoors.

## Planting Seeds That rEDefine Success

***By Evans Duren***

"If I tell you a chicken can pull a plow, hook him up!" My grandfather, who has been a farmer his entire life, said this to me hundreds of times growing up. It didn't matter if we were working on his blue Ford tractor in the middle of a field, heading down a two-lane highway with a load of corn, feeding livestock, or eating dinner around that old table in the farmhouse dining room. When he felt the need to remind me of a chicken's unexplainable ability to pull a plow, he made sure to do so. I never questioned him. The truth is, I figured he knew something about chickens I just had not learned yet. To this day, I will not bet against him on whether it is possible.

I imagine this was my grandfather's way of asking me to trust him and believe beyond what I had already determined in my mind to be possible. While the farm was a world of adventure for a young boy, little did I realize it was also a builder of dreams for a young man.

As a child, I saw the farm through the eyes of a child. I rode tractors while plowing fields, fed animals early in the morning, watched my grandfather work on equipment, delivered livestock and produce to the farmer's market, and many other things that happen on a farm. I only recognized these events for what they were in those moments. At the same time, I only saw my grandfather as a farmer even though he was an entrepreneur running his own business.

There were times I may have visited the farm during the planting season, but never saw the resulting harvest. The same is true in that other times, I saw the harvest but not the planting and nurturing that preceded. I may have ridden in the front seat to the farmers market to deliver squash, but that doesn't mean I was in the field picking or washing it before being packaged. Growing up, I often saw a beginning or an end to a season but missed the in-between where the most significant transformation would take place.

That transformation from seed to harvest is what fascinates me today. The fact that a tiny seed planted in fertile ground can grow into something of enormous size and benefit is an incredible thing to witness. Too often, we fail to realize the power of something so small, but we are given season upon season in which we can test the seed.

Think about it. Just like farming has seasons, so do our businesses and our lives beyond the marketplace. Each year, millions of US-based farmers take to the fields in hopes of producing a crop that will create a profit for their families and ultimately provide food for households across this country. Are our businesses really that different? Do we not take to our own fields each year in hopes of doing the same things? I would venture to say we do, and the parallels are remarkable.

That farm was ripe with lessons, but it wasn't until I was older that I was able to correlate the connection between it and my business. I didn't know it then, but my grandfather was teaching me lessons that I would eventually apply in my life as a husband, father, and businessman. They were lessons and principles of how to plant, grow, and harvest.

I began reading John Maxwell and studying business at Presbyterian College, and fell in love with the idea of becoming an entrepreneur. I wrote business plans for a restaurant, an international wine company, and a clothing retailer. My dreams felt big at the time, but it would be a decade more before I realized they never fully stretched me. Before following through on those plans, I decided to pursue a Fortune 15 sales career and landed a job selling medical supplies and equipment. This would prove to be the first time I would begin to see the farm with a fresh set of eyes.

My first move was to Atlanta for training with the local sales team. I split my time between shadowing other sales reps, studying operations at the distribution center, and learning customer service with another group. There was a solid foundation built during those few months, and my first opportunity to build upon it came in Tennessee. After a short time in Chattanooga, I transitioned to Johnson City, where I would operate my first business territory. There were some revenues already in place that I would inherit, but the expectation was I would grow the area exponentially into a seven-figure business.

Planning and execution would be critical if I were to be successful. I buckled down to dive deeper into our portfolio and gain a better awareness of my products and solutions. I developed an understanding of the terrain. I learned who my best prospects were and how to align my solutions with their expectations and needs. I figured out who my competition was, how long they had been in the area, the kind of volume they produced, and why they were successful. Before long, I had a plan and a better grasp of what was possible. I knew more about not just my company, but the business of my prospects and the competition.

That territory grew over $600K in the first seven months, and I was named the National Rookie of The Year for the company at our national sales meeting. The territory was fertile ground, and the harvest from that business helped my company, my household, my community, and countless patients that I would never meet but know they were cared for by the doctors, nurses, and surgeons I served.

Years later, I would leave the medical industry to try my hand at technology sales with a North Carolina based startup. I couldn't spell "IT" at the time, and this was a big stretch from where I had spent the previous several years. There was a solution we sold called "Avamar," and I repeatedly called it "Avatar" for weeks. Eventually, another rep on the team was kind enough to clue me in that we weren't selling the James Cameron movie, and I needed to learn my products if I wanted to make it in the business. A truly humbling moment in my career!

I grew in technology sales to a high production role and expanded my business well beyond what I had experienced in the medical field. The deals were much more substantial. I had more money, more recognition, and more praise. It was intoxicating, and the lessons from the farm faded into the background.

In my mind, I had become successful. I had earned a seat at the table, but all that came crashing down. It was Father's Day weekend when I received a letter that a former employer was suing me. It shook me to my core, and I withdrew in the middle of the storm. I felt a range of emotions that began with fear and usually ended with anger. This was never supposed to happen. I feared I had become a failure and wondered what my clients and family would think.

I began to look at my business, my customers, teammates, family, and community differently. In the pursuit of success, I finally realized that I had allowed myself to live by other peoples' definitions, standards, and expectations for my life. Success had become synonymous with production. My worth, my value, was tied to what I did for a living and how I ranked against everyone else. But that never seemed right and was not what I truly believed. Success was supposed to be defined by effort, faith, serving others, and living out my unique gifts, skills, and talents to make an impact in the lives of those around me and beyond. That's what it should have been, but I had fallen short.

The next year changed my life in a way I would have never imagined. I came to terms with the fact that I was in one of life's storms, and although I couldn't outrun it, I could outlast it. When the storm inevitably passed, there was no choice but to start over and get back to my roots. I needed to go back to the farm. I had to reevaluate what it meant to plant seeds so that I could produce a harvest.

Speaking with my grandfather, he reminded me that farming, like so many businesses, is about more than planting seeds or the harvest. He began to talk about preparing the soil, choosing the right time to plant, the right amount to plant, and having equipment that would allow you to do it effectively.

He reminded me that planting seeds is important, but there is only so much he could control between that time and the harvest. The seed is planted, and regardless of how hard he worked to provide the right amount of water or fertilizer, he could not force the seed to grow beneath the soil. Once planted, there would be a minimum one to two-week period when he had to trust a transformation was happening beneath the earth.

This was an invaluable lesson. We plant countless seeds in our business, but do we trust the process of transformation? Do we try to control the seed so that it will produce something of value, or do we allow it to grow and accept we can only do so much to influence the outcome?

When I first took my IT sales job, our vice president told me there would be a time in the first eighteen months that I would question myself and if I had what it took to succeed in my new role. I thought that sounded ridiculous, and it only made me want to achieve quicker and beyond anything he expected. It turns out he was right. I hit a wall about that time and began looking for another job without telling anyone except my wife. I decided if things did not get better, I would finish out two full years with the company and move back into medical sales.

Almost eighteen months to the day, I had an experience that changed my mind and kept me in technology. I had been working on a deal for several months, and it was the end of our quarter. The sale was on everybody's radar, and it was essential to our business as a smaller company still in full growth mode. It was a Friday afternoon, and I did something I had never done before. I got on my knees in my home office, praying to God about my business. I did not ask for the deal to close. I did ask that if it did not close, I would not implode, and that I would be able to trust everything would turn out fine. As 4:45 PM approached, I began to give up hope that it would happen that day.

Thirty minutes later, I received an email notification on my phone. The sound made my heart race. I opened my email, and it was the purchase order. This was the largest deal I had ever been a part of, and I will never forget going from doubt and uncertainty to absolute excitement. I had planted the seed and tried so hard to force it to grow for months, but it turned out there was a transformation happening on the client-side I was unable to see because I was not part of their organization. As much as they considered me to be a business partner and not just another vendor, I was still standing on the outside. I had to trust the process beneath the soil.

As much as I enjoy the financial gains in our businesses, both big and small, nothing compares to planting seeds that produce amazing relationships beyond the transaction. This is another place too many companies and entrepreneurs get stuck, and once again, the farm taught me another valuable lesson.

My grandfather's best friend was a man named Jack. They met when my grandfather was a young boy, and Jack was working on my great grandfather's farm growing tobacco. Their friendship lasted over forty years until Jack died of cancer. One of my favorite pictures at the farm was taken during squash season. Jack is driving that old, blue Ford tractor through the field while my grandfather works on the squash trailer being pulled behind it. They worked together for decades by that point, and a reporter included them in an article for the local newspaper.

My grandfather still talks about how good a man Jack was on the farm and with his own family. They worked together, broke bread together, and helped one another support their families. That is a powerful combination to grow a business, and at the same time, develop a genuine friendship.

No matter where you plant seeds, I hope you will spare enough to plant into your relationships and not just your sales. The business world allows us an opportunity to walk alongside others in their victories, losses, triumphs, defeats, and everything in-between. It would be a shame to miss that kind of harvest.

Perhaps the greatest lesson I learned from the farm is about my place as someone who is growing where I have been planted. I can still hear my father saying, "Grow where you are planted!" There is no doubt in my mind he learned that from my grandfather, and when I was born, they drew straws to see who would get that saying and who would own the chicken and the plow.

After my lawsuit, I realized I was in the growth stage undergoing my own transformation. I planted the seeds, but the production I saw in my business was not the harvest of my life. It was the harvest of my work for a season. Success was not a good crop or exceeding my quota. Success was found in the lives that were touched by leveraging my gifts, skills, and talents to the fullest. Success was never about me; it was about living in a way that allowed my business to enhance the lives of others, not just my own.

I have worked with hundreds of people over my career who were undergoing their transformation beneath the soil. Many of them have been successful by the standards we so often use to judge one another, yet they find there remains a gap in their lives they are constantly trying to fill. That gap lies between who they are, what they do, and why they do it. They have bought into the narrative of planting seeds that only lead to bigger deals, higher profits, notoriety, and market share. I do not consider any of those things to be bad, and I do believe we should run profitable businesses and excel in our markets, but we cannot accept profits and market share to be the sole reasons to work in our spaces.

To this day, my grandfather owns and operates *Duren's Farm* in Thomasville, Georgia. He has never been on the cover of a magazine, he is not famously known for his work, nor has he traveled the world teaching others to become a successful business owner. What he has done is show me you can make a living doing what you love, you can impact countless lives through your business, and there is tremendous power to be found in the smallest of seeds.

My hope is you will commit to planting seeds each season, that you will trust the process, and have faith in that which you cannot see. I want you to grow the most amazing fields in your business and prepare for a harvest that is too abundant to keep all to yourself.

I want you to refuse a life of being bound by the chains of someone else's definitions, standards, and expectations of success for YOUR life and business. YOU are a uniquely and divinely created individual (***Seed***) with an incredible opportunity to grow (***Transform***) and deliver real impact (***Harvest***) to those around you. Leverage your gifts, skills, and talents to the fullest and live your life fully alive!

When doubt creeps into your business and spills into other areas of your life, remember you have planted seeds of purpose and trust the transformation process. You must look forward to the harvest and know that you have prepared for this season.

Anyone can be ordinary, dare to extraordinary!

***

To contact Evans:

Website – www.evansduren.com

Email - evans.care2succeed@gmail.com

LinkedIn - www.linkedin.com/in/evansduren/

Instagram - www.instagram.com/evansduren/

Talent Concierge, Publicist & Scheduling Rep - www.talentconcierge.co / 570.906.4395

# Shanda Gobeli

Shanda Gobeli lives her life beyond her limitations. A graduate of Wright State University and a Certified Health Coach, she is an author, speaker, counselor, and health coach. Shanda speaks around the world in places like Russia, Africa, Mexico, Honduras, El Salvador, and Haiti. She defies the odds by doing all this from a wheelchair. Cerebral Palsy is Shanda's diagnosis, but it is not what defines her. Her unshakable faith and unbreakable spirit turn obstacles into opportunities. Shanda is Founder and Director of Strength of Heart Ministries, a 501c3 nonprofit organization that serves children and adults with disabilities in Haiti. She travels to Haiti with her husband once a year. She opened her own private practice in January 2019: A New Day Health & Life Coaching, where she uniquely coaches clients one-one and in groups. She specializes in stress solutions, eating disorders, weight loss, and self-care. Monthly workshops called Chocolate & Changes offer personal strategic sessions to individuals committed to transforming their health. Having experienced countless struggles, trials, and triumphs, Shanda offers game-changing methods for transformational results. She is currently pursuing a Mastery level certification in Transformational Coaching Methods through Health Coach Institute. Her passions include her husband, ministry, coaching, reading, and traveling. Shanda and Tim live in Akron, Oho with two rescue fur babies Milo and Bella Luna.

# The Other Side of Can't

***By Shanda Gobeli, CHC***

My first tattoo is a butterfly. The delicate image permanently sketched into the skin of my left arm. It's like a henna. Fake tats don't bleed. This one did. Its raw beauty emerged from the prickly invasion. The pain fulfilled its purpose, fading into the background.

Here's a snapshot of my journey.

I grew up in the 70s and 80s. Love the music. The hairstyles, not so much. My parents raised my sister and I in a loving Christian home. We embrace one another and love Jesus. Our whole family got baptized together in a YMCA swimming pool. Not long after that, I decided that I wanted to be a missionary. From then on, my life would never be the same. Being born with Cerebral Palsy, doctors predicted my future as lacking vitality. My parents didn't listen. Neither did I.

Early on, I determined to find ways to express myself. I was given a typewriter to use. My world opened up. My fingers slowly found each key as I typed poems, letters, and stories. I was placed in regular classes for English, Art, and Math. I received help with homework and my personal needs. Speech and physical therapy added to long days. Eventually I chose to stop therapy. Due to my disability, everything I do requires ten times the energy of the average person. The time had come to focus on academic excellence.

The Ashland School Board gave permission for me to attend my hometown High School. I studied hours every night. I learned to do math on a typewriter. The school installed a lift for me so I could eat with the other students. I didn't use it much. I felt self-conscious in the crowded cafeteria. Often more food ended up on the floor or on me than in my mouth. I didn't want an audience. During study halls I did my homework on a typewriter stationed in the nurse's office. I did well on my ACTs. And four years later I graduated with honors. Class of 1988.

Teachers encouraged me to participate in plays and musicals, but I practically threw up at the idea of being on stage. I did however enjoy writing articles for the school paper. I named my weekly column, "Iron Sides". I still remember my spoof on the television show, Wheel of Fortune with the blond bombshell Vanna White. I love making people laugh.

Somewhere in the middle of my Sophomore year, I began exhibiting Anorexic behaviors. Perhaps the bulk of my wheelchair made me feel bigger than I was. People would clear the way for me and open double doors for me to maneuver my chair through. It was meant as kindness. It reminded me of my extra girth. I determined to find ways to reduce my size. Monitoring every bite, eating minuscule amounts everyday was a goal I pursued obsessively. These unhealthy habits and constant hunger wore me down and increased my frustration. My relationship with God and my family suffered greatly. My only hope was knowing I wasn't going through this trial alone. At my thinnest I weighed 79 pounds and extremely anemic. Action was eminent if I didn't stop starving myself. I continued to struggle with food into adulthood, but gradually I pursued recovery. My faith took center stage again as I began to value the life I had been given.

I began Wright State University in the Fall of 1988. Would I be able to live independently? Could I carry a full class load? Did I have the courage to face a brave new world? Absolutely. I leaned into the challenges of living on my own. It was time to take initiative. I didn't want to sit on the sidelines. So, I put my shyness to rest and embraced every opportunity.

I joined the Wright State women's wheelchair basketball team. I never made a basket. I struggled to keep up on the court. My only skill was getting in the competition's way. But even with my minuscule athletic ability, it was fun to be a part of a sport. I showed up for practice and workouts and gave it all I had. Our team made it to the Finals in Los Angeles. We took last place and enjoyed Venice Beach. At the awards banquet the last night, a surprise waited for me. I received the award for Best Sportsmanship. Apparently offering apologies to my opponents for ramming into them made an impression.

I applied to be a summer missionary through a Christian organization on campus. Being accepted and assigned to serve in the

Midwest felt amazing. So with a wing and a prayer, my friend Danielle and I boarded a plane to Kansas City. We taught backyard Bible Clubs in hundred-degree heat and served as camp counselors for sixth grade boys for two and a half months. The smell of kids' dirty gym socks haunted me for weeks. My disability added challenges too numerous to mention. Some hilarious; most, not so much. But with the help of God Almighty, we completed the mission. I was hooked.

After graduating with a Bachelor's Degree in Communications, I moved to Georgia. It was hard on my parents. Even so, they drove twelve hours pulling a U-haul trailer. I learned some decisions are better than others. Working as a children's ministry leader at a small southern church did not go as planned. The pay was negligible, transportation proved extremely difficult. I tried moving closer to the church, renting a tiny apartment in the middle of the country. It just wasn't a good fit. After a year of living on Cheerios and potato chips, I went home.

However, I remained determined to work. Four months after returning to Ohio, I was hired by a nonprofit organization helping individuals with disabilities secure housing and health services. I worked there for five and a half years. When I talked with my boss about taking another job offer, she dressed me down for being ungrateful. Although it was a devastating conversation, I stayed on for another six months. On my last day, my colleagues along with the boss surprised me with a farewell party. I was relieved to be leaving on good terms.

Akron has a great public transit system. This is one of the reasons I chose to stay. I love hopping on a bus and roaming around town. As expected, riding a city bus has it ups and downs. After years of practice, I navigate the crowded isles without much problem. Being quick and efficient while entering and exiting is crucial within bus culture. I've only witnessed one fist fight while riding. And it happened right over my head! My wheelchair was strapped down, so it was impossible for me to move away. A woman sitting across from me threw herself over me for protection. Her remarkable kindness saved me from getting a black eye. She just smiled at me and waved goodbye as she got off at the next stop. People are amazed and/or dismayed when they hear about my solo trips around town. But I'm never really alone. God's protection has always been my soft place to land.

One time while I was cruising down a sidewalk, my wheelchair stopped on the railroad track by my house. I tried everything to get unstuck. I prayed that the train would be delayed. I started flinging my arms around and yelling for help. A young guy pulled over and asked if I was okay. I not so calmly screamed, "No! Not Okay! Stuck on railroad track! Need. Help Now!". Quickly he wrestled my wheelchair off the track into a grassy area nearby. I gushed my gratefulness to God and the nice young man. I then called my husband to come get me. I would live to ride another day.

In 1994, I became a member of The Chapel in Akron. Six years later they hired me to help develop their disability ministry. Families with disabilities started to come to the church. They were overjoyed to find a place to belong. I also worked as Ohio's Program Coordinator for Joni and Friends, an International Disability Outreach. I sharpened my skills as a speaker, writer, and organizer during that time. The Director and I traveled around Ohio training churches and leaders on disability issues. Our trips also extended to Honduras and El Salvador. We led more a dozen mission trips to minister to those with disabilities through wheelchair distributions.

While on staff, a medical emergency prevented the Founder of Joni and Friends from attending an annual fundraiser event in Minneapolis. I was invited to speak in her place. I embraced this amazing honor with excitement. I called my dad and he prayed for me over the phone. I had only a couple hours notice before rolling onto the stage. A thousand people came to the event expecting... not me. My dad whispered right before we hung up, "Shanda, you've been preparing your whole life for moment." I don't even remember what I said. The standing ovation brought me to tears.

I've always adored watching the Olympics. I don't like much television, but during those two weeks I'm glued to it. I never dreamed I would one day participate. My pastor nominated me to carry the Olympic torch through Akron in 2001. When I received the call telling me I had been chosen, I thought it was a prank. But it was really happening! So, on a freezing day in January, I bundled up in official Olympic garb and set out in my wheelchair. Tim said

I looked like a snow bunny. I prayed to not drop the eternal flame. More than anything at that moment, I did not want the torch to be extinguished on my watch. The community celebration connected to the global spirit of unity and overcoming. The experience was magical.

I'd never walked more than a few steps in my life. It seems God had other plans. I'd been invited to do life differently. However, at one point I craved a physical outlet for some personal angst. So, I entered a one-mile fun walk/run event. I swam laps every day and walked around the University of Akron's track using a walker. I recruited my good friend Tim (who is now my husband) to help me train. Halfway through the summer I was able to make it around the track four times, equaling a mile. I felt a rush of excitement, and the desire for a greater challenge. Within days of hitting the one-mile goal, I called Tim with another idea. The event also hosted a five-mile race. I informed him that I wanted to walk the five-mile course instead of the shorter path. Tim was understandably bewildered. He described my new target as completely unreasonable for someone whose body is not accustomed to walking at all. My simple response was, "I know. Are you in or out?' Next day we started up leveling my training by tackling hills, stairs, and uneven terrain combined with longer distances.

On go day, we started at 8:00am. My ankles, knees, and wrists were taped for support as I prepared for the moment of truth. I had accomplished three consecutive miles during training. I figured five miles couldn't be that much farther than three. Obviously, my brain had marinated in the pool too long. Family and friends took shifts to walk with me. Tim matched me step for step without a break. As the day progressed, my rate of walking slowed exponentially. Leg camps haunted me. People offered me food along the way, but neither Tim or I were interested. All I could do is focus putting one foot in front of the other. Distractions were not welcomed. I completed five miles at 5:00pm. I pushed my body for nine hours. It never forgave me for the torture I put it though that day. I'm grateful to God for the strength to persevere. And thankful to friends and relatives who supported me. Tim became my hero and my best friend that day. Little did we know this walk would lead us into a lifetime together.

My first overseas mission trip was Moscow. My friend Suzy went with me to help me navigate the unknown. My enthusiasm about being in Russia drew looks of suspicion. I greeted everyone with gusto. Someone finally told me that zealous public interaction was not the norm, especially with strangers. So, I toned it down a bit, but always slipped a smile in whenever I had the chance. I loved seeing Red Square. We visited a church in the Russian countryside. The people offered little potatoes as gifts. They still had dirt on them. The sincerity of those elderly women made its way into my heart. Humble, yet unashamed of their offering. I long to grow in humility. And to be unapologetic of what I've been given to share with the world

My passport makes me look like an international spy. Or a participant in The Amazing Race. Honduras (10 times), El Salvador (3 times), Africa (2), Mexico (2), Bahamas (1), and Haiti (8). Most have been mission trips and one or two personal outings. Traveling with a disability takes practice and patience. I am always the first passenger on the plane. I'm also always the last one off. My husband and I try to make the best of the situation. It is a blessing to be able to go global. It's not easy, but it's worth it.

In 2017, my husband Tim and I started a nonprofit organization called Strength of Heart Ministries. We traveled to Haiti a couple times with other groups on mission trips. I couldn't stop thinking of the precious people we met. A young man with Epilepsy confined with chains. A mother paralyzed giving birth to her son and then abandoned by her husband. People with disabilities existing on scraps of food, some treated like animals. We work with our ministry team and raise funds to provide daily food for children and adults. Our goal is to offer Christian love and support. Medical care, transportation, education, entrepreneur opportunities, and housing assistance are provided. Our unique approach involves going to the people who need help rather than making them come to us. My husband and I personally go to Haiti once a year. Funding for this outreach is donation based, and 100% goes to the ministry in Haiti. For more information, please visit www.strengthofheartministries.com or our Facebook page: Strength of Heart in Haiti.

Cultivating strong relationships takes priority with me. I notice the people around me and look for ways to make their day a little brighter. When others stare or ask questions about my wheelchair, it opens up a personal connection. Some encounters awkward. Like the time when I said hello to a little girl in a restaurant. She opened her mouth... and screamed. I jumped a mile. She then turned to her mother and said incredulously, "Mama, mama, it talks!" I belly laugh about it now, but it was hard not to feel like a two-headed monster. I smiled at the mom. She looked as if she was going to faint with embarrassment. All I could do is wave goodbye as she dragged her kid out the door. I didn't dare say anything else.

There are many ways to help others in this world. My gratitude is inexpressible for the opportunities given to me to make a difference. I hope that I'm nowhere close to being done. In June 2019, I resigned from my staff position at The Chapel. I had completed my training to be a Health Coach a few months before. I fell in love with this amazing new opportunity. After becoming Certified, I enrolled in the Mastery Program. I don't do anything half-way. The Coaching Industry offers a beautiful landscape for me to flourish, stretch, and grow. Entrepreneurship is a dream I don't remember having, yet it feels as natural as breathing. Every experience, trial, and triumph is woven together, creating a tapestry of faith and strength to keep moving forward.

For me, coaching is a blend of compassion and courage. I walk alongside clients as a tour guide of limitless possibilities. People go to Chiropractors because adjustments are needed. In my coaching practice, I focus on the alignment of the heart, mind, and body. I help clients who are stuck in stressful situations to choose a different response. This includes areas of weight loss, self-care, chronic stress, lifestyle illnesses, and body image. My ideal clients choose to invest in themselves like never before. They position themselves for inevitable transformation.

I live on the other side of can't. I'd love to show you around.

To Contact Shanda:

Visit me at www.anewday.name

Facebook.com/A New Day Health & Life Coaching.

## Chris Baniewicz

Chris Baniewicz's greatest accomplishment has been raising two daughters who are having successful careers. Along with a successful corporate career, Chris has been involved in entrepreneurial efforts, including network marketing.

He credits his career success to the teams of people who worked for and with him; the leaders he had a chance to observe and learn from; and the people and leaders he has met in the network marketing industry.

Chris grew up mostly in Central New York. Chris attended the US Naval Academy, where he obtained a degree in Aerospace Engineering. He had a 7-year career in the Navy, as a weapons and engineering officer. After an honorable discharge, and for more than 20 years, Chris rose through the ranks at Lockheed Martin, in a variety of leadership positions. He was most influential and successful as a program manager for large-scale projects such as weapons, fire control systems, electric ship propulsion, sonar, and radar.

In the last 10 years, working for a not-for-profit defense company, Chris led a team in the development of technologies deployed around the world, supporting governments and militaries to keep their borders and citizens safe.

Chris is very engaged and active in a single network marketing company. He is eager to bring wellness technologies to everyone, and financial income opportunities to those interested in creating a passive income.

## Daily Success Principles to Live By

***By Chris Baniewicz***

Achieving success is simple, but not easy. What do I mean by that? It boils down to a few simple things, to practice every day, and master the fundamentals. The fundamentals of how to be successful are straight forward, but not easy to follow, given today's environment of data overload, social media, and all the distractions these create. To help you, I will share four fundamental principles in their simplest terms. If you can master these, you will immediately have better results in many areas of your professional and personal lives. The key is combining knowledge, along with disciplined, personal behavior. Knowledge alone is not power. Knowledge, applied with the understanding that comes from self-awareness, is power. Success and results are what I mean by "power". Isn't that what we all strive for? Success, results, and adding value to others? To help you, I will repeat certain points throughout this chapter because they are important to achieving results.

If you look around, there are many people who seem to be successful. However, you will find they are dissatisfied or unfulfilled. In my experience, it's because they primarily focus on one area of their lives, at the expense of other areas, such as making a difference in someone else's life. When they achieve success in that area, as they define it, they still feel unfulfilled. As someone looking in, from the outside, you would never know it. Yet, headlines are filled with people who seem very successful; for example, those who are financially successful but end up tragically committing suicide. As we know, setbacks in life are often temporary. Why take such drastic measures, when you have achieved what you set out to do? We all have a chance to influence the future, with the decisions we make daily, and where we put out focus.

To achieve success and be fulfilled, at the same time, you need balance. Balance means looking at all areas of your life, including the financial aspect, your relationships, your beliefs on spirituality, your contributions to other's success among others. We don't need to strengthen them all, but we do need to pay attention to most of them. When you work on setting your priorities and deciding where to focus your energy, take them all into consideration. Be discriminating on determining what is most important to you. Do not just intellectually evaluate your priorities. Pay attention to what is in your heart and gut. I believe you gut is your subconscious speaking, which is the warehouse of all experiences and knowledge you have accumulated and will continue to accumulate your whole life. Most of us do not tap into that enough. We decide mostly on intellect alone.

We live and make decisions based on our conscious and subconscious minds. Normally, one is stronger than the other, and are not connected. When you can create a bridge between the two, leverage the two, be aware of both, and live your life based on the strength of both, you can live a more purpose-driven life, have balance, and achieve more success based on what is most important to you.

Looking at my own life for inspiration, I have not been perfect in achieving balance, but I have had more successes and positive results than failures. What I have learned is that when there are failures, you add to your gut knowledge, increasing your abilities beyond just your intellect. I don't suggest you fail on purpose. However, if you are not failing, then you are not stretching and learning. We all have a desire and need to grow. Learning through failures, taking risks, expanding your knowledge, being open to new ideas, are some of the ways to grow as a person. I hate the phrase "that is beyond physics." I say it is beyond what we understand today, but it doesn't mean it is not possible. That is how new things are discovered. That is how greatness is born. By those willing to look beyond what they are today and be more than they were yesterday. Someone once told me that if you suffer from anxiety, then you are living in the future. If you have depression, then you are living in the past. Whenever I feel anxious or depressed, I quickly evaluate my current thought patterns and get back to the moment (the NOW). Living in the NOW doesn't mean we do not set goals or think about the future. It is that we look at information as a thing – not as an emotion. Knowledge, with action, leads to success.

What I am sharing next is based on years of success and failures, feelings of pleasure and pain, and reading and learning about these topics. I am giving you my informed observations. I am not an expert, but success leaves clues. What are those clues? We all have insights into them. Wouldn't it be great if these clues, these nuggets people talk about in many words, are captured for you in writing, which is short, to the point, and with no fluff. Nuggets that you can practice every day, for the rest of your life. Something you could read every day, put into practice and be more self-aware. That is the key. I challenge you to master what is in this chapter and you will be well on your way to a balanced, successful life. To master a new habit, and I will share the four I find most useful, you need to repeat and focus on them daily. You need to keep repeating and practicing daily to master a new habit.

Fundamentals Principle #1. Focused Time Management = success. I believe that poor time management is the #1 killer of people's success, and it touches just about every aspect of our lives. What is everyone's limitation – time. We all have the 24 hours in a day. So, it is not about having enough time, but what are you focusing on. You often hear people say they didn't have enough time to do something. I will tell you that they are just kidding themselves. The real answer is that what they were trying to achieve wasn't a priority, or they did not focus on it. That's the truth. Remember, success is simple, but not easy. Simple because it boils down to three things which are tied to time management. Those 3 things are: set priorities, make decisions, and focus. However, it is not easy because we are bombarded with things that compete for our focus, especially in today's age of data overload. We think we are being productive, but if you are not adhering to those 3 simple things, you are probably not as productive as you could be. What are you doing with your time? Most people do not really know. If people really tracked their time, they would see how unproductive they really are based on what is most important to them. If you do not change something today, you will not achieve whatever it is you want. Now if surfing on the internet, binge watching Netflix, or chatting in the hallway aligns with your priorities, then that is good. But if you want more, then maybe you need to prioritize, decide and focus on something different every day and adjust. I follow these 3 simple steps religiously, and I challenge you to see if by setting priorities, making decisions, and focusing on those with discipline and rigor, it helps you achieve more of what you want in life.

A simple example are meetings. How many times have you had a nonproductive meeting? Try this. At the start of the meeting, state this is a decision-making meeting and what the outcome will be. Then lead the meeting with the focus on that objective and achieve it, instead of just blindly conducting a meeting, which often go off track. Even a meeting without any decision can be focused. For example, the purpose of the meeting may not be to arrive at a decision, but a brainstorming session, where the focus is to develop choices. You can then have a follow-up meeting to decide on which choice is best. If you follow this strategy, I bet you will have more productive meetings, with actionable results. You will also feel better after the meeting. That leads me to my next topic.

<u>Fundamentals Principle #2. Be a Visionary Leader</u>. Let me start by defining what visionary Leadership is for me. It is not just about making good decisions or giving good direction. It is lies in these 3 things:

- Seeing a vision for the future that others do not and believing it can be achieved
- Inspiring others to be better than they think they can be
- Leading a team where they are better together than apart

I often share with people that my success was the result of being proactive. Yet, when I look back, it was really based on being visionary, which also allowed me to be proactive. What do I mean by that? What I lacked in experience or technical know-how, I achieved by being ahead of the challenges and being ready when they happened. I am always ready with a plan B, or even a plan C, D, or E. People always wondered how I could make decisions quickly when things went wrong. Because I was thinking ahead. Not living in the future, but anticipating, evaluating, and ready for when things went wrong -- and they will. This also ties to time (schedule). Time is as much of an important element as is data. If you aren't prepared, you take longer to make decisions and when time runs out, you may be forced to make a suboptimal decision. The more proactive you can be, and the more ready you can be, you can save time which also gives you more available options to explore. If you stop everything, wait to decide, you lose those options and your runway. Although I believe that to be true, but I also believe it is an important trait for a leader, to combine “resourcefulness” to the mix. People will blame the lack of resources for failure. Lack of people, money, capital, etc. Although real, leaders succeed despite those resource challenges, because they are resourceful. They find ways to fill gaps. Keep doing that and you will get better at finding how to leverage the resources you have. You will also get more comfortable with it and expand your gut. As a leader, you need to see where you end up before others can see. You also need to have an undying conviction of what it is, and that you will get there, as a team.

As a leader, you combine time management (focus), Ego, and EI to understand, feel, and motivate individuals to be better than they may currently believe. You not only create a vision for the team, but you see the potential of each individual. The uniqueness of everyone is what brings value to a team, along with the understanding of each team member. Not trying to mold everyone into a the same individual but move every to a common vision by leveraging their uniqueness. If you can understand each person and their strengths and weaknesses, then you begin to build a cohesive team that can thrive individually, and as a team, with common vision. Individual strengths, leveraged by a leader with a clear vision, makes for effective teams. The team needs to believe in the leader and everyone on the team, no matter the differences. It is a leader’s job to facilitate this. A leader is an influencer.

Let me close this topic with an easy way to determine whether you are a good leader or not. It’s simple. Do people work with you, follow you, and listen to you because they must or because they want to? If they want to, that is a sign of a good leader. So, occasionally, ask yourself that question to monitor you progress as a leader throughout your career.

<u>Fundamentals Principle #3. – Nurture a healthy Ego.</u> Too often, when you someone complains about bad behavior, they’ll say it’s their ego. Having an ego is neither good nor bad. We all have an ego, and I believe it is the number one reason we behave the way we do. So, to me, the ego is either healthy or unhealthy. It is better and

more productive to have a healthy ego. Ego can change and evolve, but the first step is awareness. To practice awareness of your ego, whenever you do something or say something, especially to someone else, ask yourself why you said or did that. If it was only self-serving or you have an ulterior motive, most likely it stems from an unhealthy ego. Did you purposely say something to hurt them, to get only what you want, or just to be mean? If it wasn't those things, then it was likely a healthy Ego. But, the most important part of all of this is knowing yourself, why you do what you do, and to be self-aware. By recognizing, learning, and adjusting you can nurture a healthy ego. Most people go through life just reacting, without understanding why people respond to them a certain way and the consequences of their actions. With each interaction, practice and pay attention to the how and why of what you are doing. This allows you to be more self-aware, which then provides a better result and awareness to improve. The importance of self-awareness ties into my next principle, which is Emotional Intelligence (EI).

Fundamentals Principle #4 - Strive to be an Emotionally Intelligence (EI) individual. Too often I hear people say, "Boy, I had good EI because I kept my temper". EI is not about how well you control your emotions. We are creatures of emotions and we do not want to be emotionless. I believe the core of EI is self-awareness of your emotional state. The quicker you understand, use, and manage your own emotions, the better you can interact in the moment and be more effective. It might be best to delay a decision or an interaction, if you recognize that you are in a certain emotional state. Effective EI allows us to empathize and connect with people at a much deeper level, and to live a more authentic, healthy, and happy life. So, learning to recognize is the first step. Many people don't have this skill. As you get better at it, it also becomes part of who you are. It takes time and practice. Be more self-aware. That is the key to EI. An example would be for anyone with children. You may be furious of something they have done. You confront them in anger. You aren't listening or in the moment, but you keep on moving forward with the conversation. Most of the time, nothing effective comes out of it. But, if you cognize your emotional state, you may want to come back to it when you are operating from a self-aware position and can communication more effectively. Most of us know when we angry, we don't think or behave the way we should, and often, are not proud the outcomes. We are usually disappointed or regret the way we acted. This all takes practice, but it is a great principle to master.

<u>Final words</u> – For me, it's not about where you start, but where you are heading and the person you become during the journey. We will have many destinations during our lives. Moments of constant decisions, and redirection, no matter how subtle. Live life in the moment. Be true to your decisions, priorities, and passions. Give yourself a break when you make mistakes or make a bad decision. It's part of the growth, and it helps provide that gut knowledge to help you make better choices. It's all part of the journey. My recommendation is for you to photocopy this chapter and carry it with you always. Read it repeatedly, until these fundamentals become daily habits. Then extend your knowledge deeper into each one of these areas, but only after you have become a master of the basics. You aren't what you were yesterday and tomorrow you will be a different person. The future is not determined, nor written in stone, but is constantly flowing with our daily decisions and actions. Live in the moment. Be more in tune to your subconscious (gut). You will be amazed at how much more you see and hear. You will attract more energy. You will be more aware of surroundings. We all have greatness in us. Find yours. Share yours. Be great.

Parting Quotes

- Constantly work to be a better you and good things will result from this focus.
- There are only reasons, not excuses.
- Intelligence, talent, and fortitude are great, but often these aren't what separate the great from the average. Instead, the difference is in our daily habits whether conscious or subconscious.
- When there is a day, there is a way. Success is not about having the resources, it is about how resourceful you can be, with what you have.

- Remember, the path towards greatness and success, can be achieved by daily actions and decisions made. Why not start today?
- Life is change; growth is optional.

***

To contact Chris:

baniewiczchris@gmail.com

http://www.chrisbaniewicz.com

http://www.leveragedprosperity.info

## Sara Plinska Camilo

Sara Camilo is the owner of Camilo Careers, LLC. She's a Certified Professional Career Coach and a Certified Professional Resume Writer.

Camilo Careers specializes in helping early and mid-career professionals in finding a new job, determining their next career move, and discovering a new direction in their career. Her mission is to inspire individuals to find the best career path for themselves, their strengths, and their drive as well as guide them on how to navigate social media and the technical online world.

Sara has 15 years of recruiting and corporate leadership experience working for various organizations, agencies, and Fortune 100 companies. She has helped many individuals create a high-quality resume, negotiate the salaries of their worth, and guide them to a fresh happiness in landing the best new jobs for them.

Additionally, she has coached clients in developing their interview skills, some of which resulted in receiving job offers within 24 hours of their final interview!

Sara grew up in West Allis, Wisconsin, and currently resides in the greater Los Angeles area. She found success quickly in the entrepreneur industry and shares some noteworthy lessons within this book. Check out the chapter, "A Career with a Twist."

# A Career with a Twist

### *By Sara Plinska Camilo*

Before taking the step into entrepreneurship, I had 15+ successful years of navigating the corporate world. I advanced through the recruiting industry; therefore, I met, interviewed, and offered jobs to many professionals who were genuinely enthused to accept these offers. Personally, I established life-long friendships and made unforgettable memories. Yet, something vital and valuable was missing. I was missing the satisfaction.

This experience bestowed on me the knowledge and expertise to guide individuals into the next step in their careers. The switch to Career Coaching has allowed me to evolve from a productive employee, getting the job done well, to feeling rewarded in my career, and the architect of my future.

I'm still a novice when it comes to entrepreneurship; yet, I have already learned a great deal about this craft, and I enjoy sharing it with future entrepreneurs.

**Entrepreneur Lesson #1:** Everyone has something unique to offer.

When I initially considered becoming a Career Coach, I worried that this form of coaching would be a short-lived trend, and it would not have the capacity to become a sustainable career. I was making a solid six-figure salary in my job at the time, so I asked myself, *"Would I even match that salary long-term?"* Doubtful.

Fact: I am exceeding that salary in my first year as an entrepreneur.

Yes, I am grateful to have the skills built over the years to apply to my company and to share and divulge with my clients. My corporate past has allowed me to relate in some capacity to every situation and each challenge clients have brought to me.

However, I similarly learned valuable skills from other entrepreneurs who have minimal-to-no experience in the corporate world. Gaining fresh perspectives on careers, business, life, and entrepreneurship are extremely beneficial. Everyone is unique and has something to offer. This lesson is what makes entrepreneurship so exciting, beautiful, and exceptional. Don't find yourself in a scarcity mindset; it's a limiting place to be for any entrepreneur.

**My background:**

As mentioned, I started my career as a Recruiter. I eventually learned executive recruiting, and I managed teams of recruiters. I have over nine years of experience managing people. This valuable experience developed my skills as a leader, a decision-maker, and a motivator, and I apply these skills regularly into my business and with my clients.

As a Recruiter, I enjoyed interviewing candidates, speaking with these professionals about their goals, and listening to what they strived to do next in their careers. I recruited and hired talented individuals in multiple industries including retail, engineering, operations, IT, and marketing. Consequently, I enjoyed learning about various industries, and how they operate together and separately to be successful in their realm.

I learned what effective resumes should look like across industries, how to be a strong interviewer, how to use LinkedIn, how to get that offer, and how to negotiate salaries. This knowledge defines the foundation of my business today.

Throughout my years recruiting, I had many friends and family reach out to me to gain my insight on promotional opportunities, to refresh their resumes, and to help them handle those awkward salary negotiation conversations. I truly enjoyed helping my friends in their career paths. Plus, my success rate was off the chart! (I was often rewarded with a rum and coke with a twist of lime…it's that *twist* that makes the drink extra tangy, refreshing, and satisfying.)

Yet, as I progressed in my career in recruiting, I noticed a switch in my mindset.

While in my day-to-day job I was hiring talented professionals into their dream jobs, my gut was telling me that I wasn't in my *own* dream job. I wasn't happy in my job anymore, and I hadn't been for a while. I switched jobs and switched companies; yet, these changes brought only temporary happiness. The underlying problem was that I knew I was in the wrong career.

I went through phases of giving myself morning pep-talks just to get to the office, to too many Sundays extending the weekend mindset and avoiding preparations for the workweek. I knew I was miserable, and I didn't know how to fix it.

The basis of my unhappiness was personal. Many professionals flourish in the corporate world; yet, I didn't anymore. Instead, I felt increasingly constricted and limited in my job year after year. The corporate structure felt suffocating. I knew I needed a pivotal change, and I dreamed about owning my own business.

With these gut-wrenching thoughts, another question came to me when I considered career coaching as a new path: "*How am I going to coach people in their careers when I couldn't even coach myself?*"

I didn't know this at the time, but my work experiences, doubts, and insecurities were preparing me to coach others going through the same challenges as I had. Now, I'm particularly grateful that I pushed my way through those ordeals and learned from them all. The lessons learned from my own journey are a piece of what makes me a successful career coach today.

Being an entrepreneur is fun, it's exciting, and it's what you make it for yourself. The possibilities are endless, which is hugely motivating to me and is what makes me work hard seven days a week.

**Entrepreneur Lesson #2:** Know your strengths and apply them.

When you work for a corporation, each employee's performance is reviewed annually. No matter which company I worked for, my manager at the time would provide me the same piece of feedback: *One of my strengths is building relationships with people.*

It was a consistent piece of feedback throughout my career. Initially, I didn't think much of it. I didn't think this strength held much weight. I took it for granted and only saw the benefit of it at parties and social events.

Then, after hearing it a few times, I began to recognize it and believe how valuable this skill could be for me. Both over the phone and in person, I was comfortable talking to people, I built trust and ease quickly, I enjoyed helping people, and I naturally made people smile.

Eventually, I figured out how to use that skill for my benefit and the benefit of others. Clients come to me with frustrations and challenges; in turn, I quickly build rapport, gain their trust, and genuinely guide them on the best path for them and their careers. This strength, along with sharing the knowledge I had gained, has brought me to the place I'm at today with career coaching. Knowing your strengths increases your confidence and success.

**Entrepreneur Lesson #3:** Don't wait; take a risk and make a change.

I became exhausted complaining to others about my job situation. I truly believed that if I complained enough, someone would hand me the solution to my problem on a silver platter. Well, guess what? That's not quite how it works.

Instead, this complaining created more stress, anxiety, and extreme frustration in my life. I had more frequent migraines, drank more cocktails, lost more sleep, bought more Powerball tickets (I have yet to win!), and just became infuriated with myself for feeling so lost, and not taking action.

I knew that I needed to take control of my career, even if it was just a baby step. At this point, I had been following several entrepreneurs on LinkedIn who had built careers around resume writing. So, I decided to pursue this path as a *side hustle* to see how I enjoyed it. Subsequently, I became certified in resume writing through the Professional Association of Resume Writers and Career Coaches (PARW/CC).

As soon as I listed this new certification on my LinkedIn profile, I was contacted by multiple companies who were hiring resume writers. It was exciting to see this demand! Eventually, I accepted a contract position with the fantastic and progressive company, "Inside Recruiter." With them, I was given the flexibility to write two resumes weekly to enhance my writing skills on the side of my full-time job.

For over two years, I worked many nights and weekends consulting with individuals on their resume needs and career goals. Doing so made me realize the following:

- Social media is intimidating when it comes to searching for a new job.
- Networking and communicating with recruiters online is uncomfortable and awkward.
- Those who feel stuck in their jobs don't know what to do to feel unstuck.
- Many people have LinkedIn profiles, yet, don't know how to use that resource to their benefit.
- Even sales executives don't know how to sell themselves in their resume or in an interview.

This list could quadruple in length, and yet, when dealing with clients I had solutions for every problem. This was my arena. I knew what to say, how to advise, and how to help. It was easy and fun.

Essentially, these early clients helped me prove to myself that I had an abundance of knowledge and techniques to share with others, and I loved sharing this expertise to benefit their careers.

It's important to keep another factor in mind: Since 2018, the unemployment rate in the U.S. has fallen to 3.5%, making it a new 50-year low, which makes the job market more competitive than normal.

With this awakening, I knew what I needed to do. It was time to turn my side hustle into a business. I was already building it in my head for months; yet, I was terrified to leave the cushiness and the consistent paycheck of my corporate job to make it happen.

Finally, I stopped playing ping-pong in my head and I took an enormous risk: I quit my day job to turn my capabilities and expertise into a coaching business.

When I resigned for the last time, it felt different than any other resignation and it felt right. From that moment, I haven't looked back. I felt empowered, inspired, and motivated to get started. Today, I'm the proud owner of Camilo Careers, a career coaching service, guiding individuals across the U.S. to own their careers and find their drive and happiness.

A future goal is taking Camilo Careers internationally. As an entrepreneur, I'm privileged to aim high and have nothing to hold me back.

**Entrepreneur Lesson #4:** Research, collaborate, and do more research.

I used multiple resources to help me build my business, and I still use them today. The top six resources and recommendations I have for new entrepreneurs are the following:

1. Join freelancing and entrepreneur groups on Facebook.
2. Watch relevant YouTube channels, and collaborate with entrepreneurs inside and out of your industry.
3. Invest in entrepreneurship training and certifications.
4. Find personal and business mentors; invest in their services if you have the means.
5. Join LinkedIn Groups and industry associations and interact with fellow members.
6. Refer to LegalZoom.com for legal documents and questions.

The list doesn't stop at these six, do your research and find more helpful sources for you.

**Entrepreneur Lesson #5:** Learn what structure works best for your success.

Entrepreneurs work uncommon hours, especially when getting established in their niche and when the company is expanding. I'm currently writing this chapter on a Saturday while watching my Wisconsin Badgers play football. I actually thrive in this environment. I expect to work some late evenings and occasional weekends; yet, I have unlimited vacation days in this new job, which makes everything acceptable! Perhaps your Saturday mornings don't have the same flexibility because you are running to a child's sports activity, volunteering at your local community center or training for a race, but the beauty is that you get to choose when to put in the energy.

On the contrary, if you thrive with a routine, the lack-of-schedule I portrayed probably makes you squirm. As an entrepreneur, you get to set a schedule that works best for you. It takes trial and error to determine what schedule, process, and flow work best for you. It's important to stay organized, strategic and task oriented. Gone are the days of bosses checking in with you for a status update (thankfully!)

**Entrepreneur Lesson #6:** Be disciplined and establish deadlines.

It's easy to work every day when you love what you're doing. Therefore, the discipline I'm referring to is around follow through and client experience. If you have a scheduled call with a client, call them on time. If you tell a client you will email them a helpful resource, email it to them immediately. The last impression you leave with a client is just as critical as a first impression.

As a business owner, executing creative ideas and strategies are your responsibility. It's easy to let a day go by, and then a week, and you're still planning or strategizing these ideas; meanwhile, no online action or social media branding has occurred. Yes, I've been there!

Setting clear deadlines for execution is the critical first step; then, even more critical is step two, which is the meeting those deadlines. Today, proactive planning is vital to any successful organization, and many apps such as Hootsuite and Planoly have been developed for this purpose. Check them all out. These apps help you to work smarter, not harder! Use those accessible resources to build your successful business.

**Entrepreneur Lesson #7**: Just do it, even if it's tricky and messy.

I love this lesson. As a rookie entrepreneur, it has challenged me the most, and I wouldn't be where I am today without this pushy advice.

To break it down, beginning as an entrepreneur will be clunky. You can have all of your processes, templates, ideas, and timelines in place; yet, do not expect them to operate smoothly 100% of the time. Be prepared to make tweaks along the way. You will make edits and revisions for days, weeks, maybe even months.

You're constantly learning and growing, so don't wait for everything to be perfect and flawless before you launch it. If you do, you may not execute a single idea. And, if you don't execute your ideas, you will have $0 in revenue coming into your bank account.

So, the advice here is to just do it, try it, launch it, send it, post it…and then perfect it in motion.

**Entrepreneur Lesson #8:** You will not please everyone.

Everybody likes a people-pleaser, right? Well, if you're a people-pleaser, you will be forced to change that personality trait as an entrepreneur, which can absolutely be done (I am living proof).

I have accepted that I am not the best Coach for everyone I connect with, and not every person is the best client for me. Not every sales call or cold email will convert into a client. That's okay! I do not take it personally.

Believe it or not, I have had prospective clients that I have turned down, and it will probably happen again. I'm an extremely competitive person, so I often want to take on the challenge of helping everyone who crosses my path, but I'd be naïve to believe that I could. It's the reason why I'm not the only Career Coach in the world. I'm not the right fit for everybody. I know that if I personalized these business transactions, I'd be prone to compare myself to other coaches, and I don't allow myself to go there. That's how the phrase "imposter syndrome" was coined.

I approach each sales call and new client reminding myself that I'm the expert in my field. I believe I can help many people, and I know the best types of clients for me and my business; therefore, I'm interviewing each client in the same way as the client is interviewing me. Stay strong and trust yourself; doing so makes for a truly effective coaching experience.

Life Lesson: It's simple…it's your life, take control.

This chapter ends with another inspiring example to change careers.

In 2018, I took a magical trip to Africa. The trip was momentous not only because I got married while I was there; but because I was captivated by the people we met who were so genuinely happy and so giving of their joy. They smile constantly. They hug tightly. They live a simple, "Hakuna Matata" lifestyle while having so few possessions or modern conveniences. I found this coolness extremely inspiring and moving. ("Hakuna Matata" means "no worries," just like in the movie, *The Lion King*).

At this time, I was still in my corporate position. In that job, I was spending a considerable amount of time in a miserable, toxic state of being.

This journey in Africa, the people I met, and the conversations I had, made this trip a significant inspiration for me to take control of my happiness and my life. Part of my mission with Camilo Careers is to inspire others to take control and live their finest life.

Being an entrepreneur has allowed me to help individuals find their happiness by enhancing their careers and their lives. I offer the following support and solutions through Camilo Careers, LLC:

1. Updated resumes for a new job or career.
2. Interview preparation, and how to bring your best package to the conversation.
3. Techniques how to search for jobs online and determining the best jobs to pursue.
4. Training for LinkedIn and building a strong profile.
5. Tips and a pep-talk around the dreaded salary negotiation conversations.
6. Managing a career change, for those who want to break into a new industry.
7. Let's not forget about college students and recent graduates! I have built "The Gold Package" dedicated to them and their career plans.

Please check out CamiloCareers.com to learn more about me and my organization, how to make that change, and do it now. It's your life, take control of it.

***

To contact Sara:

Sara Plinska Camilo, CPCC, CPRW

Certified Professional Career Coach

Certified Professional Resume Writer

Camilo Careers LLC

www.CamiloCareers.com

Sara@camilocareers.com

https://www.linkedin.com/in/sara-plinska-camilo/

# James Hyde, MA

Jim has 31 years of policing experience and retired as a Police Chief. Jim has a Bachelor of Science Degree in Criminal Justice from the University of South Dakota, a master's degree in Clinical Psychology.

He is a graduate of the University of Southern California's Delinquency Control Institute and the Senior Management Institute for Police sponsored by Harvard University and PERF. Jim is a certified Executive Coach and doctoral student studying Organizational Psychology.

Jim is a co-founder of the *West Coast Post-trauma Retreat*. WCPR is a trauma treatment program for emergency service professionals. He was the board president of the *First Responders Support Network.*

He was the *California National Guard's Embedded Behavioral Health Program Coordinator* and lead trainer for the Peer to Peer Combat Stress Program and a recipient of the United States Army's Patrick Henry Distinguished Service Award.

Jim is the lead *U.S. trainer for Different Tracks Global* of Belfast, No. Ireland. DTG is a global non-profit organization providing community-based conflict management leaders across around the globe.

Jim was a trauma & conflict presenter at the UN Peace Conference at The Hague, Netherlands. Jim was a co-recipient of the 2010 U.S. Department of Justice Project Safe Neighborhood's *Community Outreach National Award.*

# The Journey to a New Calling

## Building "The First Responder Retirement Academy"

***By Jim Hyde, MA***

Hitting the Wall

After 31 years of law enforcement, I hit the wall. The Great Recession of the 21st Century had taken a toll on our California city and me. The city was on the verge of bankruptcy and I was the Police Chief of a sinking ship. We had already reduced the police department's workforce by 45% through lay-offs and retirements. Many of the neighborhoods across our city that we had taken back from crime were now being surrendered back to the criminals.

I was burned out. My wife found me sitting in our living room at 2 am trying to figure out ways to save jobs. I had only slept 2 to 3 hours a night for the past year. She could see the wear on my face and body. Susan looked me in the eye as I sat there and said, "The job is killing you and I need you to get out, I don't want to be a widow". The 2$^{nd}$ thing that I loved the most, being a police officer, was the thing that was slowly killing me.

I had been in the cardiac care unit a month earlier for three days with chest pains and high blood pressure. The cardiologist who discharged me from the hospital said, "I think it's time you find a new profession".

After three decades, I had lost 38 of my first responder colleagues to murder, suicide, accident, and catastrophic medical events. I had attended 104 first responder funerals. I had spent two thirds of my life away from my family on the mission of protecting other families. It was time to refocus my purpose, passion and calling in life.

### Step 1: Refocus My Life

It was also time to fix my tired body. I had already had 11 broken bones and 7 surgeries from work related injuries. I had also delayed reconstructive surgery on my shoulder for two years to keep working to protect our city. So, I told my City Manager that it was time to have surgery to repair my shoulder. While I was off work for two months healing from surgery, I started exploring what my next purpose and mission in life would be defined as.

I told my wife that I would start the retirement process from policing. I knew that I had more to contribute to the profession. The first responder career had given me a proven set of problem-solving skills that could still benefit others, but I soon discovered there was no clear roadmap or blueprint to find the way to my new life.

So, I started the journey to find my new normal of a healthy way of living and growing. Susan and I began to study the best practices for an active and meaningful first responder retirement. Our challenge was, how could you go from 120 MPH lifestyle for decades to a 60 MPH lifestyle.

My wife Susan and I have spent over three decades working with first responders and soldiers across the country who have been suffering in silence. Five of our law enforcements colleagues had taken their lives due to Post-Traumatic Stress Disorder (PTSD). We couldn't just stand by and watch that continue to happen. We had to do something to help the wellbeing of our first responder and military brothers and sisters.

We had developed a series of trauma recovery programs or "best practices" designed to help those struggling with PTSI recover. We had implemented these interventions in a variety of ways through trainings, trauma retreats, peer support programs and embedded behavioral health programs.

Across America our Spartan guardian brothers and sisters were suffering at alarming rates. For every law enforcement member killed in the line of duty, two to three more took their own lives. An EMT's average career only last eight years before they burn-out and leave their honorable profession. Firefighter trauma numbers were going up too.

**Step 2: Finding a New Purpose**

The three decades I spent as a policeman, including a stint as police chief in two different California cities, seemed only a preamble to the new work that I was supposed to be doing. I started exploring my work options. Because of my education and experience in trauma psychology, I was approached by my military friends to enlist in the California Army National Guard and go to Officer Candidate School (OCS). They needed help to reduce the growing epidemic of soldier PTSD and suicide. The years of fighting the war on terrorism were taking a toll on mental health resources, which happened to be one of my skill sets

OSC was an applied leadership program. It required an intensive level of performance by officer candidates, more than basic soldier training affords. Basic training teaches recruits to do everything from brushing their teeth to the correct way to sit, stand and march. A great deal of OCS training consists of challenging candidates with a series of complex problems, expecting them to work as a team to solve them to complete the exercise.

One of those problems, for example, was the Leader Reaction Course (LRC). Recruits in boot camp are faced with an obstacle course consisting of walls, ropes and running. The LRC obstacle course, on the other hand, combines the basic obstacle course with complicated problems the team members (squads) must solve. Each problem involves a unique obstacle. In each case, we had to devise some way to get ourselves and our equipment from one side of the impossible obstacle to the other. Success always requires teamwork, planning, and communication.

Unbeknownst to me, OCS was giving me a new set of leadership skills and business management tools. I was learning how to lead and build a small business with a clear direction and mission. I thought I'd learned a lot as a police officer, but OCS added another layer of applied business knowledge.

After graduating from the Army OCS program, with the nickname of "Dad", I was assigned to the Behavioral Health Unit. I was given the nickname by my classmates because I was the oldest OCS candidate. The unit commander assigned me to help implement, expand and manage two combat stress programs.

I was back to being busy, in fact as busy as during my career as a cop. I continued to pursue a passion that was an important part of my life during the past three decades of my service as a police officer. I was helping reverse the growing challenge of PTSD and suicide among soldiers deploying and returning from the Middle East battle fronts.

## Step 3: The Birth of a New Business Idea

Several years earlier, my wife had started interviewing pre and post-retiring first responders concerning their transition plans to retirement. The common denominator she found, was that for most, there really wasn't a plan other than going camping and fishing. She found that the recently retired first responders were struggling in several aspects of their early retirement.

They were suffering with anxiety and depression because they had lost a sense of purpose in life and a loss of professional identity. She discovered that individuals in high-performing professions place a significant amount of emotion and energy into their identity and status in society. These recently retired first responders were also struggling with significant health issues that had been left untreated, while the first responder was working full-time. A common trait for the first responder culture is to be strong and push past your personal problems to support the mission of protecting their communities and supporting their comrades.

Members of the first responder professions, whether currently in uniform or not, differ in fundamental ways from the civilian population they serve. Those serving or have served in uniform share a similar set of beliefs, attitudes, and behaviors that we can refer to as the "Culture of the Uniform". For the most part, people outside this unique culture are not aware of its existence.

The life-or-death environments that first responders operate in don't allow for many mistakes. The intensity of such expectations leads to continual self-evaluation of performance. Right at the beginning of a first responder's career, the academies pound the standards of perfection and continued improvement into recruits, which never ceases throughout their career. The low tolerance level for mistakes and errors, means that they are going to do everything they can to learn from any mistake so that it will never be repeated.

They force themselves to live by a professional and personal code of conduct that extends beyond mere perfection into another core value of the "sacrifice". People in uniform put themselves in harm's way and accept their potential injury or death as an inherent part of the profession. So, protecting and serving others is another core value of the uniform culture.

A subset of this culture is the expectation of extended absence from your family. My own career working patrol, narcotics, gang suppression, and homicide caused me to spend days at a time away from my family. At one point in my career, it extended past physical absence into emotional withdrawal. Many times I would be so exhausted when I finally made it home that I would walk right past my waiting family to my bedroom that I had made into an isolation chamber with aluminum foil covered windows, so I could get a few precious hours of sleep.

Another part of the "Culture of the Uniform" is a warrior mindset that stands them in good stead by reinforcing courage when confronting adversaries who offer continual threats of injury or even death. There is a downside, however, that results in their needing our help. The same warrior mindset that helps them stand up to threats also makes it difficult, sometimes, for them to ask for help, since they imagine that doing so is tantamount to an admission of weakness. One of our ongoing challenges, therefore, is to help the uniformed person to understand that everyone needs help, at one time or another, and that not asking for help when you really need it, is not a sign of strength or of courage.

**Step 4: The First Responder Retirement Business**

The Harvard Business Review published a study on the impact of retirement on high performing professions. They stated, "People tend to identify strongly with their work, their disciplines, and their careers. Many (retirees) wish to learn, grow, try new things, and be productive indefinitely. These feelings can be especially strong in policing, where officers, at all ranks, talk about the camaraderie and sense of purpose that they do not see in other professions."

First responders are great planners at work, but not so great on the home front. The demanding career of a first responder usually comes first and family second. Our research shows the first responder retirement is a major life event. For some, it is a critical incident. Everything he or she represented in the world suddenly comes to an end. For the majority of first responders, there is no farewell luncheon or "thank you for your sacrifice and service" ceremony. You are just out the door.

The huge first responder locomotive just keeps rolling down the tracks, but you are no longer on it and it keeps getting smaller as it moves away. Suddenly, you are alone. This newfound loneliness may result in depression and trigger memories of traumatic experiences long buried. A first responder must have a plan for a successful retirement.

Within weeks after retiring from the active first responder community, you go from confidence to questioning your decision for leaving the career. Within weeks you are basically forgotten by the organization. They will waive and say hi to you in passing when they see you, but you're no longer on the team roster. The retirement transition significantly impacts your physical, emotional and mental well-being. You poured out your heart and soul for 30 to 40 years to the first responder mission, missing family birthdays and holidays, and now you have a significant loss of value and purpose in the world.

For many people, retirement can feel like suspended animation. The symptoms can be unstructured time, a sense of idleness, boredom and for some, depression. First responders work and sacrifice for decades to get to the retirement prize and to their surprise, arrive at an unnamed and empty wilderness location. They thought there would be a simple trail map waiting at the trailhead with their dream retirement lifestyle.

Key retirement planning tasks are to establish a new personal identity and find ways to replace the sense of belonging, like the one you had as a first responder. There are other losses to be dealt with, such as; the loss of purpose, influence, importance, and excitement. It's a big adjustment!

**Step 5: Finding the Right Business Recipe**

After spending most of my adult life working in government, I had no idea how to start a small business, let alone grow it into a successful business. I talked to friends, interviewed other small business owners, looked at business management school programs, and researched the web to find business coaching companies. I was looking for a business coaching company that had an ethical track record, was proven to delivering concise and clear business methodologies, and was available when I needed their experience to get past a significant hurdle.

After months of searching, I saw a Facebook ad for a business coaching and conference speaker mentoring program called Industry Rockstar Global Mentorship Program. They offered a free 90-minute introductory seminar in downtown Sacramento, California. I thought, why not check it out. I had been to several other 90-minute sales seminars over the course of the past 20 years. This one was different because the seminar speaker, Kane Minkus offered conference speaking tips during the seminar, instead of the usual sign up, pay and we will give you the secret sauce of business success later.

After the seminar presentation, I was so intrigued by the great business tips and genuineness of the speaker that I signed up for a 3-day business coaching conference in San Francisco a month later. When I attended the conference, I discovered small business owners and fledgling entrepreneurs like me, looking for their new purpose and path in the world. I saw outstanding presentations by very successful entrepreneurs like Kevin Harrington from the Shark Tank TV show and Les Brown, rated as one of the top three motivational conference speakers in the world.

The various business entrepreneur conference presenters opened my mind to a new world of opportunity. They showed me a powerful way to help retiring first responders create their personal retirement lifestyle blueprint for the next 2 to 3 decades of their lives. My wife and I could now build a business system to significantly reduce first responder post-retirement depression, divorce and suicide. We would be saving the lives of the lifesavers!

**Step 6: Saving "The Lifesavers"**

Today, we work with pre and post retired first responders who don't have a clear direction for their retirement. These purpose driven men and women are now preparing themselves for their next life achievements. We help them build a blueprint for their next meaningful journey.

Through the First Responder Retirement Academy, we help America's retiring first responders discover a new mission and purpose for their life. They get a blueprint to build their next active 30 years. They find they are happier and more content because they have meaning and purpose to each day. They can contribute again, which is who they really are internally. They plan their next personal legacy.

The following testimonial from a 30-year veteran women Police Officer told us that we had successfully found our next mission and business:

"Hi Susan, I just can't tell you how much I enjoyed the Retirement class that you and Jim presented. It truly relieved much of my anxiety and gave me a roadmap to success in my future pursuits after this stage of my working life. Facing the challenges of retirement from law enforcement head-on with all the pathways that you both brought to the forefront gave me a newfound confidence in jumping into the next stage of my life.

Before the class, I was so stressed out about retirement, that I wasn't feeling good about the end of this juncture. At 58 years old (next month), I knew I couldn't continue this way like a [spring chicken]. I was afraid to pull the plug. As we get older, we just have to face the music that we are not in our 20's anymore. To remind myself of this very fact, I just had to laugh about being the oldest woman out on patrol as I start to feel new aches and pains... LOL. Thank you both so very much!"

**Conclusion: Don't Try This at Home… Alone**

We were lost on how to build a successful, let alone a nationwide business, until we signed on with the Industry Rockstar business mentorship program. We first tried to build a new business at home and alone. For years we just could not get any real traction until we started looking outside the four walls of our home.

The Industry Rockstar business mentoring program has made a significant and positive impact on our lives and ultimately the lives of retiring first responders and their families. The variety of business topic workshops, online live teaching sessions, individual coaching meetings, and online training videos and materials are well done and applicable. They gave us a clear and detailed entrepreneurial map to building a successful business and healthy lifestyle.

***

www.FirstResponderRetirement.com

info@FirstResponderRetirement.com

https://www.facebook.com/events/338356163737620/

Business Line (916) 895-1536

# Zahra Karsan

Author, Speaker, Certified Success Coach, Founder & CEO, GetZENd. Certified in Mindset Coaching and Neuroscience, Zahra is a trusted Success Coach to dozens of global executives and a Public Speaker. She is the best-selling author of *How Do You TAKE YOUR HAPPY? and REWIRE for HAPPINESS,* and is the creator of the REWIRE System, a groundbreaking methodology that retrains your brain for greater happiness, health, wealth and success.

Her company, GetZEND, offers a suite of products that include online video training and an award-winning App to help you stay on track with your goals. With over 20 years of experience as a Management Consultant and Corporate Coach, goal setting and producing results became second nature for Zahra.

She now coaches corporations and industry leaders on how to achieve their life goals so they can Live Better.

Zahra also works on her passion project with Honey Shine Inc and The Steve & Marjorie Harvey Foundation to empower young girls to move past limiting beliefs so they can live more powerfully.

# How to Unstop Yourself

***Zahra Karsan***

Did you know that we evolved to be good at *survival*, rather than happiness, health, wealth or success? In fact, our very nature works against our attempts to achieve those things. We are actually wired to *protect ourselves*, flee from fear and danger, and keep ourselves safe. Much of this activity happens below the surface, beyond our awareness, in our unconscious brain. There are patterns that get triggered and they get automatically activated, without our even knowing, as though we are on auto pilot. These patterns can sometimes be effective in helping us deal with tricky situations, but oftentimes, they are there to shut us down, keep us disconnected, all for self-preservation. They stop us, have us struggle, even fail at times… even if they don't stop or slow us down in one area of life, they will likely affect us elsewhere. We may, for example, excel in our careers, but something is lacking in the area of love, family, health, finances or in some other aspect of our lives.

We try so hard, don't we? to be the best at everything we do? to be happier? to find that secret place where we can finally feel *at peace, yet accomplished*, feel like *we can have everything we need AND do it with a sense of ease*. We stumble through our lives, first as children, as students and as friends, then we try to be the best adults, leaders, co-workers, parents we can be, but it's not always easy to wake up each day feeling rested, energized and able to conquer the day ahead. Oftentimes, we feel tired, stressed, worried about whether we can get to it all. Without even realizing it, our own unconscious patterns work against us to cause us undue stress. It's like we have this undercurrent of worry that accompanies every thought, every activity throughout the day. When we think of a new challenge or goal, these worries plague us, slow us down, remind us that we haven't been able to charge ahead and achieve these goals in the past so why try now? So *we get stuck...* we get *stopped* in our tracks from creating a life that would really excite us. When this happens, we stay in the comfort zone, where it's safe and we don't take the risk. The problem is… we are biologically wired to have purpose and meaning and, in order to follow a life that aligns, it requires us to push past these patterns. In fact, when we allow ourselves to be *stopped,* we become increasingly frustrated, dissatisfied, unhappy and live in a state of dis-*EASE*. We try even to find some escape from the displeasure of not living our best life and often we choose the wrong things to provide some temporary relief. We may think we connect deeply with people and yet, many of us still long to feel closer, more loved or just have a deeper sense of belonging. We work hard and do well in our careers, but still long for more financial wealth or security. We want to have real financial freedom and independence, maybe even be an entrepreneur but we don't know where to start… and so, we don't. These are just some of the ways our unconscious patterns do not work in alignment with what we truly want for our lives. So… if this all happens beyond our conscious brain, *is it possible to learn how to access the unconscious brain* so that we can feel more alive and choose behaviours that steer us *toward* happiness and success versus away from it? Is it possible to find ways of rewiring this programming so that we can be happier, healthier and wealthier?

We have all tried to develop new habits in past but with little success. Think of all the failed diets, exercise routines, financial goals, new years resolutions!

The most exciting research from the world of Neuroscience lately is around the idea of *Neuroplasticity.* It says that the brain is not static in nature, but it is, in fact, *malleable* and, therefore, *changeable. This is the biggest breakthrough there's been in decades*! And it can be applied to life so that we can be in a better state of health, live life with more ease and be happier!

Research shows that if you want to make a change in any area of your life, we have to uncover the path to create *lasting change* and now we finally know how to do it! We've uncovered real scientific evidence of *neuroplasticity AND precisely how much time it takes to change the brain.* Neuroplasticity is where the brain displays signs of *enduring change* and there's real evidence now of *precisely HOW* to produce lasting change and we can create this change in just 6 weeks! You can now learn how to rewire your brain for a happier, healthier, wealthier and more fulfilling life, with more energy and vitality, less stress, better sleep and you will feel *lasting* changes so you can live better.

Success used to be defined in terms money, wealth and power. Most people today realize that successful living includes happiness, health, wealth, love *and purpose*. If we were to summarize it in a new way, then *HAPPINESS is an active process through which people become aware of, and make choices toward, a happier, healthier and more successful existence.*

People ask me all the time: "How did you get here? You seem so calm, happy, self-assured and you take action like very few people I've ever met. Can you share what you do or how you got here?" I realized that my unconventional education and career path provided a diverse range of tools and they helped me access greater joy, better sleep, better health, greater focus, financial success and way more fun than I'd ever had before! My experience as a management consultant and my education includes leadership and success training and studies in psychology, positive psychology, neuroscience and how to access and then *rewire the unconscious mind.* As I tried to answer the question "How did you get here?", I realized it was challenging to guide someone through this without taking them through the very same 30 year journey I took to arrive here. I'd like to also share with you that this journey was not just straight to the top. There were *a lot* of ups and downs over many years. There were countless painful challenges that forced me to observe the good, the bad, the funny and the ugly of who we are and what we need to do to align with who we are meant to be. There was failure after failure in my business until I discovered my purpose was to educate and to transform lives. I initially built an app that included many of the tools I use in my daily routine to help people stay on track with their goals and keep their vision clear. If you can't envision it, you can't design it. If you're not crystal clear on your goals, then how can you accomplish them? If our fears influence our actions, then our thoughts and behaviours all stop us from doing what we intend. When you envision your goals, *you have to be able to see yourself completing them successfully,* just like an athlete before the big race, or they'll never come to fruition. *You have to be so diligent with your thoughts and raise the amplitude of that vision in every way till you get the desired outcome.* The GetZENd App was designed with this in mind. When we released the app, it was voted One of the Top Ten Apps in the world in the Better Life App

Contest (Apps to improve the quality of your life). I was thrilled when I released the GetZENd Performance App and thought I would run an app business! Marketing an app, though, is quite a different thing and it's a high-risk business unless you have huge investors behind you. I also had a successful coaching business, thinking I would continue to do coaching and run the app business separately. It was in marketing both these businesses that I realized my real vision. My real purpose was to use all I'd learned to transform lives and help bring healing, health, wealth and success to those who struggle to achieve their dreams. While at the time, I had no interest in becoming a speaker, I realized, if I want to effect real change, *I'm going to need a bigger platform*. I would have to *become a speaker* to really reach people and I needed to become an educator. Much of my research was on the study of success. I asked the question: "what separated those that *dream* from those that are *able to achieve* great things?" Both groups of people take plenty of action, but there was something different in the mentality of the group of people that were able to accomplish their goals successfully time and again. It all came down to *mindset*.

I realized that what we really need is *a methodology we can use to create long lasting change in our mindset,* and we need to make sure it's one that helps us accomplish our goals and bounce back quickly when we get derailed, because *we will get derailed.*

I decided to create a system myself to teach people how to shift to a success mindset and create long lasting change in their lives. I call this system The R.E.W.I.R.E System and it consists of six modules, each designed to help *rewire the brain* so you can be happier, healthier, wealthier and more successful in your life. The REWIRE System is taught across several platforms from the book to a live workshop designed to teach you how to think, feel and act differently. In the workshops, I get to see people transform over the course of a few days and step into a more powerful version of themselves! (For our events calendar, please go to www.getzend.com or www.therwiresystem.com). I also do this work with non-profits and teach children how to live more fearlessly. It's beautiful to see kids just come alive again after life has dimmed their light. We all come into this world so bright and ready to conquer any challenge and then life has a way of knocking us down, creating fear, and having us protect ourselves. Those patterns again.... the ones that stop us.

We evolved to be on alert for danger and we have a built-in mechanism known as fight-or-flight that helps us navigate to safety quickly. In past, this used to be required to flee from predators and when we found safety, our brains quickly signaled our bodies to return to our calmer state. For us today, because life is so busy, our fear response is constantly being triggered by stress and worry, as though we are in real danger. The critical issue is, because life is not slowing down for us, we are barely able to return to a state of rest quickly, if at all. Over time, we have strengthened our response to stress and fear and have weakened our ability to return to our natural state of rest and CALM, precisely the opposite of what we truly need.

Prolonged stress wreaks havoc on the body – although it helps us accomplish great things when we are running on adrenaline, it also shows up in the form of high blood pressure, chronic fatigue, poor sleep, poor health, a weakened immune system. So... how can we reverse this cycle when it happens so automatically? Is it possible to retrain our brain to return to our natural state of calm and have a more fulfilling life?... The answer is, Yes! It is possible to learn how to rewire your brain and finally accomplish your goals!

Let's talk about how. Our brains communicate by sending chemical signals called neurotransmitters between nerve cells across the synapse. The release of neurotransmitter is determined by patterns of electrical activity or neural impulses. These neural impulses encode our thoughts, actions, experiences and feelings. *Everything we think, do, feel and experience gets encoded over neural pathways.* The important thing to note, is that these pathways are not *hardwired* in the brain. They can change over time, *based on what we choose to experience*. Everything we do, think, feel and experience then reorganizes the function and even the structure of these neural pathways. As we repeat thoughts, actions, feelings and experience over time, *we can actually change these pathways.* We can make them stronger or weaker. Our brains do this involuntarily for certain things. For example, in a recent study of ballerinas at the Imperial College London, it was found that, as they learned to dance, their brain began suppressing the response to become dizzy. It's as if the brain learned to disregard it during the dance so that it could focus on other, more necessary tasks to perform the dance. *It weakened the otherwise normal response* and *strengthened* other responses. This is one of the ways the brain responds efficiently to the world around us. Imagine if we could actually *choose to lessen the negative responses* to daily stresses and *instead* react in ways that serve us better. Let's say you were training to be a public speaker - let's say it was something you've wanted to do but was always afraid to do. Some of what you'd be feeling as you got up to the stage could be anxiety, fear, excitement, nervousness, faster hear rate - and all that goes with the nerves of doing something totally out of your comfort zone. Now, *imagine if you could have more control over how you felt* as you walked up to that stage? What if you could retrain your brain to *pay less attention to the fear* and *more attention to the excitement* and even *choose to feel CALM,* poised, and confident instead? When particular events happen in our lives, they trigger certain emotions and the biochemical release that goes with those emotions. Sometimes, the emotions we want are there, but there are others that show up and either slow us down or stop us from truly achieving what we desire. We now have proven techniques to retrain your brain to respond in a more favorable way when these situations occur. By training your brain for greater calm, less stress and greater focus, we can reduce the *power* of the negative response that stopped us in the past. *We can learn how to move past those negative responses and retrain the brain to move forward instead.*

In the same way as with the case of the ballerina study, we can *choose* to strengthen or weaken particular pathways that interrupt our happiness and our ability to achieve the success we want, so that we operate in a way that would be more *effective.* There was a Neuropsychologist, named Donald Hebb, who first used this phrase in 1949 to describe how pathways in the brain are formed and reinforced through repetition. It's called Hebb's Law and it states that "Neurons that fire together, wire together". Over time, performing the same set of actions repeatedly, fires off the same neural circuit, strengthening the synaptic connections and that neural circuit then begins to wire together.

The most recent evidence out of Harvard University and Imperial College London shows that neuroplasticity - the brain showing signs of *enduring change* - actually *sets in* between days 35 to 40. At day 37, we can see map changes in the brain and cortical reorganization. This means that *the optimal time to create lasting change in the brain is six weeks!* We *can* change how we *think, act, feel and behave* so that we achieve *anything we believe we can have!*

Using this research, we can apply it to how we process the world around us, and we now know that *we can create true change in our lives.* Six weeks is all it takes to be able to create enduring change in the brain. So how do we use this knowledge to create powerful and positive change in our lives?

Incorporating studies in positive psychology, the subconscious mind and neuroscience, the REWIRE system trains you to restore your natural, calmer state, so that you can operate more efficiently - have an improved state of health, better sleep, greater focus and productivity and you'll also lighten the way you feel on a daily basis, so you are less stressed, more easily back to balance when life events do come up and have more freedom from worry. In just six weeks, you'll weaken your response to stress and retrain your brain for greater calm, better health, more wealth, more joy and fulfillment and you'll begin living a more successful existence!

If I could sum up all I've learned that got me to this wonderful place in my life I would say the following…

1. The greatest gift we could give ourselves is to acknowledge our weird and wonderful ways and still find a way to enjoy the ride!! Acknowledge how brilliantly your body serves to protect you, but don't let it stop you.
2. Surround yourself with a tribe of people who have done what you want to do, because they did the research, made the mistakes and can help you navigate.
3. Get coaches to help get you there so you have the right tools to set yourself up for success!
4. If you fail, get back up and try again. All you need is six weeks to instruct your brain to say YES I CAN and change your life!

5. Most importantly, NEVER EVER settle for a life that's less than you deserve! REWIRE and have the life of your dreams!

***

To contact Zahra:

Website 1: www.getzend.com

Website 2: www.therewiresystem.com

## Colleen Duggan

Colleen Duggan has launched many successful entrepreneurial ventures, including a successful wholesale furniture business she and her late husband founded. She is a distributor for Young Living Essential Oils, and a licensed and certified trainer for B.A.N.K. (the only methodology in the world scientifically validated to predict buying behavior in less than 90 seconds). She is also involved in a leading-edge company with a breakthrough frequency healing and pain control class 2 medical device doing business in over 50 countries around the world. In addition, she represents a company that markets several break-through products including a powerful coffee that promotes weight loss. She loves to volunteer in her local community and beyond. Colleen lives in Vancouver, Washington. She is widowed and has a married son and three grandchildren.

## We'll Figure It Out!

### *By Colleen Duggan*

I remember hearing myself telling, Ahmed, my Clark College foreign exchange student from Saudi Arabia, those words many times. He laughed, we laughed together. We still repeat that mantra when we talk today. We had to figure out how to help him buy his first car, negotiating with the car dealership and with each other. I was able to teach him to drive in the snow since he'd never seen snow before. We were grateful, and we always figured it out.

I realized that that has been one of my life mottos that had served me well throughout my life and continues to do so today. My long-time friend, Kristi, often reminds me that I frequently say how fascinating I find the solutions.

There is ALWAYS a solution. Thinking outside of the box, changing the size or shape of the box (sometimes it's a circle, a triangle, or even a balloon), and creativity is paramount to success. Fine tune the art of listening, REALLY listening. Solutions may be hidden in the lines in between someone's description of a problem. Often, we are too busy concentrating on how to respond to them rather than hearing the solution.

The solution often comes when we are quiet. We have two ears, two eyes, two hands, two feet, and ONE mouth for a reason. Jack Canfield said recently that it was during his quiet meditation time that an audible voice told him his book series he was formulating in 1993 should be called "Chicken Soup for the Soul". The rejection part of the story (144 publishers turned him down) is very long and very fascinating. However, the tenacity and creativity finally implemented ending up providing incredible financial, emotional, and spiritual benefits to millions.

I grew up in a seriously religious home where education was not always recognized for its value. We were all, 1 foster son and 4 daughters required to go to one year of Bible school. Curt to find his wife and we girls to get our MRS. Degrees. The premise was that if two people believed in God and prayed hard enough a marriage would work. That theory was not successful for me in my first marriage. Adding the other components needed proved much more rewarding for Jim and I in our marriage.

We had 6 ½ years of immense pleasure, fun, hard work, and all-around bliss, while running our S Corporation in the furniture business, and spending a lot of time in the beautiful San Juan Islands relaxing on our wonderful 34-foot power boat. But as the roller coaster of life was happily gaining momentum, four months after we were married, Jim was diagnosed with multiple myeloma (a relatively rare cancer that develops in plasma cells, white blood cells that grow in bone marrow). The doctors we first saw did as much as they could and then they referred us to Fred Hutch Cancer Research Center, which is a teaching hospital and at the time rotated their doctors once a month that came from all over the world. We endured unbelievable and barbaric chemotherapy and complete body radiation treatments in Seattle, that were excruciatingly painful, at times humiliating and so damaging to his body. We eventually did the double bone marrow (stem cell) transplant. Since he did not have a donor, his stem cells were harvested by hooking him up to a dialysis machine. The machine spins at a rate that extracts the stem cells from one arm and returns the remaining blood product through the other arm. The stem cells are then purified as much as possible and then frozen until the treatment begins. All treatments were outpatient except for a few nights in the hospital. The one night I stayed there with him we had a fire drill! . All medical personnel were teams of people who did the best they knew how 20+ years ago. I am grateful that today's treatments while still difficult are less harsh. And that progress has been made and the pendulum is finally starting to swing to preventative maintenance in our society rather than trying to treat diseases and the damage that a lot of toxic medications cause. I am not against the entire medical system. There are thousands of lives saved every day by the men and women doing surgeries and taking care of people. I'm just suggesting we reverse the process, starting with oils and other naturopathic remedies first and medicines as a last resort.

When I first entered the work force after high school, think F.W. Woolworth's in the candy department, I found I loved, numbers, customer service and chocolate. Of course, the seed of being attracted to numbers was planted by Mrs. Scanlan in Algebra in the

$9^{th}$ grade. Numbers mind you, not taxes. I liked the order of making numbers balance. I taught myself the ins and outs of payroll and the benefits that often go along with that department, government funding for schools, general accounting practices, real estate and stock market investing in various jobs I had, wholesale furniture sales where the territory I had with Jim, and for some time after he passed away, was Washington, Oregon, parts of Idaho, Alaska, British Columbia, and Alberta. In all the genres, I LOVED the customer pieces of the puzzle.

I am now educating myself in Young Living Essential Oils and replacing the toxins in my life with pure plant-based goodness. Essential oils are carefully extracted from trees, flowers, herbs, rinds of fruit, and other parts of a plant. Before getting involved with them I had mistakenly believed that essential oils were only for defusing. Oils are the bridge to natural health, there is no science to master, no fancy techniques to learn. The work has been done for you by God creating incredible plants. Oils can help with confidence, balance, sleep, immunity, stress, happy bellies, healthy breathing, aches, focus, and the list goes on and on. I love the education I'm getting, the results (essential oils support your body at a cellular level). Keeping your body moving frequently is also important, it doesn't have to be rigorous activity, in fact stretching is often overlooked for its many benefits of both body and mind. Everyone's body has a breaking point of how much it will tolerate. For some people it metastasizes as migraines, for others it's indescribable pain, or swelling and inflammation, skin issues, depression, anger or inability to sleep. Some of it is emotional, some of it is physical. Investigate making healthier healing choices and see where it leads you. Of course, what you eat and how you treat your body is also paramount to your good health. Sugar is as poisonous as cocaine and the documentary on how a certain company addicted the world to sugar is very disturbing to say the least. Try giving up one sugary food each week and see how much better you feel, and when you do indulge in small amounts of sweet treats, they will be much more enjoyable. Our bodies are designed to heal themselves, but what we often do to them undermines healing. You contradict a clean lifestyle if you use oils and eat poorly. I am fortunate enough to have fabulous grocery stores close enough to me that I can almost shop daily for the fresh foods I want to eat. The top ten most dangerous chemicals in our homes are found in air fresheners, cleaning supplies, dishwasher detergent and dish soap. Other danger spots include beauty supplies and personal care products, hairspray, gel, shampoo, and deodorant. This information is from the U.S. environmental Protection Agency's Chemicals Study. I love the creative, intelligent and inspiring people I'm working with. The loving support, the generosity and integrity of the company is delightful, and I even get to visit the farms throughout the U.S. and other countries where the plants are grown and processed. Every day, all over the world, the experts on Young Living's farms are capturing the power of the plants and putting them into a bottle with their amazing seed to seal guarantee.

I am also a newly certified trainer for Bankcode. San Francisco State University has published a white paper executive summary that scientifically validates why this methodology of cracking a person's personality code and predicting their buying behavior in 90 seconds or less and is a breakthrough that shortens the time to close a sale and increases volume. Personality profiling has been around for decades and decades, but this system teaches uses of reverse engineering, the concept of deciphering personality types in a way that specifically categorizes people according to how they buy or decide to say yes during the sales process. It teaches the triggers and tripwires of each personality type. A marketing company in California has determined that for the first time in their history they have discovered that there isn't anyone who cannot benefit from this information to enhance both their business endeavors and their personal relationships. The founder worked many years developing this buyology and when it was so successful, she explained to her boss why they needed to train everyone in the company to use it. Unfortunately, he was not an open minded individual and wanted to keep it for their personal use only. Being a wise and generous person, Cheri actually quit that job to be able to share her knowledge with anyone and everyone. It was a major setback for her financially at first, but of course the story is spreading and benefiting many people. We are currently in over 40 countries and growing rapidly. Les Brown says Bankcode is a game changer. Cheri has shared the stage with Tony Robbins, Robert Kiyosaki, Sir Richard Branson and many other leading-edge thought leaders. The company has recently added Artificial Intelligence components to its arsenal led by none other than Neil Sahota, the founder and creator of the famous computer "Watson". Applying "Why They Buy" to any person's life will give them more income to buy the Tesla they've had their eye on, or to contribute more money to their favorite charity that is dedicated to making our world a better place and saving the world for future generations.

ALWAYS try new things. Volunteer for different opportunities in your community. One day as I was coming out of a local grocery store, where a group of girls were selling candy bars. I incorrectly assumed the Girl Scouts had added candy bars to their product line. But my inquiry led me to finding out about Sea Scouts. I had not heard of them before, but they were looking for adult volunteer leaders. And that's how I ended up on many great excursions, including a two-week trip in the San Juan Islands on a state-of-the-art sailboat. A generous owner wanted to give a memorable trip to three Sea Scout girls and three volunteer leaders. I took my crab ring along and taught them how to catch, cook, crack and eat fresh crabs. For my 50$^{th}$ birthday I gifted myself 50 new adventures for the year. I had no idea that it was going to be one of the best years of my life. I also had no idea the places it would take me. Some of my favorites included riding in a fire truck for the first time. My son is a firefighter and when they are getting ready to put a brand new fire truck in service, they do many trial trips before it is actually a part of the fleet. Taking the six-month training required to become a Stephens Minister which is a wonderful organization that teaches people to walk beside someone going through a crisis in their life, not fixing them or their problem just walking through it with them. I went to 52 new restaurants and tried 52 new wines I had not tasted before. I was able to go on a once in a lifetime trip to France and Italy to different cooking schools for three weeks with a one-day layover in Amsterdam on the way home. We flew into Paris and toured the founder of French Impressionist Paintings, Claude Monet's beautifully restored home and peaceful gardens that are an explosion of color and fragrance. I even drove the twelve-lane roundabout in Paris! A Baron from Normandy who was a private chef in Seattle led us through France setting up classes with friends of his who owned restaurants and hotels. We got to take cooking classes at Cordon Bleu in Paris and were treated with special care since Bertrand was a graduate from there. Little did he know that it would be the beginning of a lucrative part of a new career for him. We ended our French excursion in Nice, France, where we turned in our rental cars and boarded a train for Milan, Italy. Most of our time in Italy we stayed in a villa in Tuscany and went to various excursions each day, from cooking classes to olive oil tastings, to wine tastings, and lunch in the home of a gracious Contessa. We also took a train to Cinque Terre, a string of centuries-old seaside villages on the rugged Italian Riviera coastline. We drove to Lake Como, Florence and on to Venice, visiting many of the islands there before taking a boat to the airport for the trip home. There were nine women on the trip. We took a year to plan it, and not once did we have any conflicts with each other, what an amazing group of women! After that I began volunteering at the cooking school in Edmonds, Washington where we all attended. It was a for profit business run by volunteers, where we got paid in fabulous food and wine. I joined the Columbia Tower Club in Seattle. It is still in the tallest building in Seattle and looks down on the Space Needle, with spectacular views of most of Seattle and the surrounding areas. They have exceptional interesting, enriching and unique events there for members. The events include social, cultural and a high-tech conference center for a business-friendly environment. They also have a world class fine-dining restaurant. They are part of a group of 200+ other country clubs nationwide, including athletic clubs, city clubs, stadium clubs and golf clubs. I was able to attend a reception and have my picture taken with the Blue Angels (but I'm still working on getting a ride in one of their planes). I even threw my own 50th birthday party there. I invited 100 people and 80 were able to attend. It was both an exhilarating and exhausting year because I was also working full time. However, it was so much fun that I decided to continue the tradition with a few important modifications. I did sixty new things between 50 and 60, but giving myself ten years to accomplish them, a mere six new adventures per year. I will turn 70 soon and will have added 70 new adventures by that birthday. I sometimes know about events in advance, but I always leave plenty of room to edit the list. I am enjoying the challenge so much that I plan to continue the tradition for the rest of my life!

Live outside of your comfort zone with a healthy balance of comfort zones in place. When you get stuck or life just seems tougher than usual have a significant list of rituals that can bring you joy to draw from that can get you back on track. They can be as simple as taking a short (or long) walk, a candlelight bubble bath, calling a friend that always "gets" you, tapping (EFT), finding something to belly laugh about, or remembering the best moments in your life. They can also be longer activities like pedicures or manicures or complete spa treatments, taking an all day road trip to either a place you've never been, or to a place that always makes you happy, making plans for something in the near future that fills you with anticipation and rewards you for getting back on track.

ALWAYS be curious, about everything. Curious about learning more facts about things you already know about. But especially curious about new things you know nothing about, you never know when that stored information will serve you well. Curiosity will take you on trips and adventures you might never have dreamed possible. Be curious about people, figuring out why they do what they do, sometimes when they don't even understand themselves.

Be curious about emotions, yours and other peoples as well. Lean into the discomfort they sometime produce and push through to new revelations. Emotionally hooked vulnerability is very courageous and clearing up misunderstandings is a kind and brave empowerment. Learn and practice understanding and taking responsibility for your emotions so that it is as natural as breathing. And remember to breathe deeply. Shame is not a productive emotion. You will have regrets in your life, but embrace them rather than shaming yourself, regrets are nothing more than a fair but tough teacher. Healing does not depend on other people, although there are many significant healers in the world that can help with the processes. Learn to craft love from heartbreak. When people show you who they are, believe them. People often make up stories because they feel threatened because all they really want to do is survive. Challenge most of those stories because they are not based on facts and can be very dangerous because they promote a lack of worthiness, lovability, and creativity in our selves or others. Often when we read a reaction in another person, we create a story that is completely false or may have nothing to do with us, but something else they are going through.

Cultivating GRATITUDE is a crucial part of a life well lived. There is always something to be grateful for. Keeping a gratitude journal is not only helpful when you write in it, but rereading it sometimes years later reminds you of all the good things that have happened in your life. Write down all the things you appreciate in your life, appreciate at least 3 people every day and don't forget to appreciate yourself! You will see benefits of attracting more abundance and joy into your life.

Start here, start now, live out your wildest dreams, splurge, dare, challenge. And, please, be kind to yourself.

***

To contact Colleen:

206-719-3159

Irishsunshine60@gmail.com

www.bankcode.com/colleen

youngliving.com/distributor/17950974

# Karin Lubin, EdD

Karin Lubin, EdD, is a coach, trainer, and leadership consultant driven by a desire to inspire and energize people and teams through the power of love, self-reflection, and inner leadership. She uses passion to catapult people into a life full of deep meaning and purpose.

After a career as a public-school teacher, administrator, and leadership consultant in diverse communities, she became the Global Director of the Passion Test Programs, assisting individuals, businesses, and young people seeking meaningful and fulfilling lives. Karin's lifelong passion for deep self-discovery and connecting others to their brilliance guides all of her work and creative endeavors.

Karin collaborates with transformational leaders and mentors to create wisdom journals that support people in transition and recovery to greater clarity, self-esteem, and emotional resilience. She uses her Seasonal Wisdom Journals™ in her quantum wisdom coaching (visit www.seasonalwisdomjournal.com or www.karinlubin.com ). She lives with her husband in Santa Fe, New Mexico.

## Be an Agent of Renewal When Everything is Falling Down Around You

***By Karin Lubin, EdD***

As a global society and as individuals we are standing at the edge of a precipice. Will we fall to our death or will we fly? What will it be for you? What if you could not only fly but become an *agent of renewal* for yourself, others, and the planet?

We're experiencing a tragic meltdown in many aspects of life as we've known it. This crisis point can be viewed as an archetypal initiation in which we've become severed from what we know and have been flung into a world in which the very sources and security of food, water, air, and shelter are threatened by rapidly changing climate. Droughts, floods, and wildfire are frequent. Social unrest, extreme inequality, political upheaval, assassinations, mass shootings, and technology used to propagandize, polarize, and tear us apart are all social symptoms of this breakdown. The effects on our mental health are apparent among those affected by threats to life and limb, financial instability, and poverty—often the trigger for mass and sudden migrations. There is an epidemic of mental health issues for young people: one in three teens today has a diagnosable anxiety disorder. Stress and depression in college students is leading to higher drop-out rates. Any sense of safety and security has grown shaky. Our assumptions or beliefs about what our lives will be like in the future are all in question.

We cannot keep doing what we've been doing and expect different results. We need to change—both our actions and the beliefs they spring from.

Try as we might we can no longer do business as we once did. Steve Farber, long-time business entrepreneur and author of four provocative business leadership books says, "Do what you love, in the service of people who love what they do." Perhaps an idea which once felt so far-fetched—bringing *love* into business—is not so crazy after all. It's true that when all else fails, it's love, the missing ingredient, that can remake, reweave, and rebind this unraveling world. I would add to Farber's statement: *And create businesses with an awareness of and compassion for how it impacts our shared world, so you can pass on a livable planet for generations to come.*

But how?

This initiation, what I call a *Global Hero's Journey* follows the archetypal hero's journey described by Joseph Campbell, the renowned professor and author who studied mythology and comparative religion. The hero leaves the ordinary world, faces and overcomes an assortment of trials and challenges, and returns to contribute what he or she has learned to the greater community.

Our current shared global journey begins with the descent into the depths of everything we fear, facing our own terror of having to change, and our own lack of connection to people and the earth. So many people feel alienated and dead inside. Perhaps you have felt this too, felt you've lost your "juice" with your work and your purpose, or are scared to raise a family because of the chaos in the world. Maybe you wonder if the children in your life can possibly have a better future. Perhaps you can't figure out what really brings you joy.

You are not crazy, and you are not alone. So many are on this journey.

Our hero or heroine's mission now is to meet these trials and challenges by growing a renewed sense of resilience, groundedness, confidence, and connection to one's inner self, a spiritual core that is always there.

I want to share my experience of my journey and how I'm supporting my clients with this new awareness. Later on, I'll outline six things that you can do to support yourself, your clients, and any you serve with this archetypal perspective and knowledge.

Maureen Murdock, a psychologist and author of *The Heroine's Journey* describes our predicament. Most of us are experiencing severe fragmentation in our own inner worlds, a reflection of what we see in our external worlds. We've lost touch with our own emotional regulation, resilience, social skills, how to communicate honestly with one another, our connection to ourselves, and to the natural world.

What is painfully apparent is that the dominant paradigm of extreme masculine power and control has created separation both within us and between us, throwing us and the entire world out of balance. When I look down into the collective chasm of despair, I see my own fear of loss and loss of control. I can feel a deep sadness at my own fragmentation and lack of connection to a living and alive world that includes people, animals, and plants that are already extinct or on the brink. And instead of facing this despair head on, I notice how I can numb and distract myself.

Seeing my own journey as one version of this larger one provides me and my clients a more hopeful and enlarged perspective. As a woman, I totally bought into the male-oriented and rational world of hard work and achievement. I was a successful teacher and administrator in a public education system for more than 20 years. I made a conscious decision to "climb the ladder of success" so I could have a larger impact in a leadership role. I slowly came to the realization that a large part of who I really was, my essence, had been suppressed. I experienced fear and a lot of second-guessing myself. My cup was running dry. Thankfully I didn't turn to the popular numbing agents of alcohol or drugs, but I was anesthetizing myself with denial, nonetheless.

Concealing my intuitive and creative side to meet impossible institutional demands began to drive me crazy. In a masculine-energy-dominant world these qualities were undervalued, and I believed that to be a responsible leader meant conforming to everyone else's expectations. Now, of course, it's really no surprise to me I burned out and began my descent into my own kind of underworld. Serving in my last administrative role I was surrounded by colleagues who'd become ill, some dangerously so. This was part of my wake-up call. Awareness slowly seeped in that I had rejected important parts of myself and not allowed my passions or these parts of myself to fully develop. I had turned away from my creative and imaginative heart and mind even as they were screaming at me to listen.

So, beginning my own heroine's journey in earnest, I began to explore a very different path, one in which I could reclaim the feminine energy of intuition, creativity, and spontaneity. Going through my dark period allowed me to tune in to my inner muse and really listen to what she had to say more than ever before. And when I did, my life completely and totally changed.

As I speak with clients and colleagues around the world, again and again I hear that we have gradually grown to accept the daily turmoil and manipulative fake news about our world and each other that is running a global society that is so over-masculinized and out of balance. I hear that there is an overwhelming need to integrate healthy feminine *and* healthy masculine principles at both individual and global levels.

What might we experience if we follow a new path of inclusion and integration of these healthy male and female principles? What might our world feel like if we related to one another with respect, honor, and appreciation. Imagine a world of respect and compassion for all persons, all bodies, all shapes, all sizes, and all colors, one in which our indigenous and conscious elders can pass on the wisdom of the ages. What if unconscious consumption and destruction of habitats and species came to be seen as completely unnecessary as we meet our needs in ways that mimic nature in its infinite creativity? What would happen if equality and opportunity for all was the norm?

An *agent of renewal* then, is one who participates fully in this vision. They lend their passion, compassion, skill, experience, and high sense of purpose to the integration of ancient wisdom with sustainable solutions in order to bring our world back into balance. An agent of renewal become a player in a global orchestra of people and institutions working and playing together to create something that is lyrical, stable, sustainable, and satisfying. This becomes our most worthy hero's journey, to rise to this challenge and opportunity, both individually and collectively.

I am excited to tell you that amidst the chaos, change is happening. As our personal journeys reflect the collective whole, more people are waking up to the potential of becoming agents of renewal. In my work, I see people no longer willing to settle. They are becoming more conscious of how their connection to their inner worlds of thoughts and feelings is a critical step to taking the most effective action in their lives. Then they become more keenly aware of the short-term *and* long-term consequences of their actions to shift our world to become one we can all live in more peacefully and bountifully.

Perhaps you or someone you know has had their own hero or heroine's journey descent like the one I described. The common theme is loneliness, a loss of connection to yourself, and an over-identification with your roles and responsibilities. Instead of feeding your inner spirit with kindness there is a denial of what you want. Whatever success might mean to you, ultimately it does not fulfill you. Perhaps you have achieved great things—yet still feel an emptiness inside.

I will outline six stages (there can be more) in the hero or heroine's journey and invite you to more consciously embrace them on your path to healing, connection, renewal, and integration.

The hero or heroine must embark on their journey individually. No one else can do it for them. Yet, as I've said, we are not truly alone as we are now on a shared collective journey and much collaboration is needed as we all learn how to navigate uncharted waters.

*The Illusion of Success* creates a *sense of loss, or spiritual death* because of a lack of connection to your soul or life purpose. You have lost touch with what nurtures you. This experience often leads us—whether male or female—back to reclaiming the feminine principle: receptivity, intuition, vulnerability, feelings, and true courage.

*The Descent* involves exposing the dark, scary, and unfelt feelings, opening to grief, rage, and disillusionment. This is where our global collective is now. It is often a chaotic experience and not the least bit happy or fun. We can sabotage ourselves from fully feeling these difficult feelings and cover them up with alcohol, drugs, sex, food, and other forms of addiction. If we knew that this step precedes movement to the next stage, we might be less resistant and more open to allowing ourselves to pass through it.

*Healing and Reconnecting to One's Whole Self* involves identifying and letting go of old stories and programming that have caused our suffering and the split that occurs between head and heart in an over-masculinized world. We begin to create new healthy habits as we open to witnessing our thoughts and feelings. We rediscover natural rhythms, the wonder and healing balm of Nature.

*Deep Healing of the Feminine Within* grows as we acknowledge our full connection to nature. We are further nurtured when we honor and reclaim lost parts of ourselves. We celebrate the juicy, wise, creative, powerful, nurturing, compassionate, procreative, courageous, sexy, and bold self, revealing and rediscovering our lost feminine power.

*Healing the Wounded Masculine Within Us* transforms the one that has taken over and diminished all things not rational or reductive, objectifying or thingifying everything. The healthy masculine is generative, playful, creative, supportive, strong, respectful, resourceful, vulnerable, loyal, and honors body and spirit.

The final stage is the *Full Integration of Our Masculine and Feminine* aspects. Harmonizing these aspects within ourselves requires reaching for higher levels of integrity. This very personal integration impacts all of society—including all social structures such as government, business, the family—through how we treat one another everywhere on a daily basis.

All human enterprise and business need to constantly shift and change to meet the needs of the customers and clients they serve. Collectively, there is a need to move through these stages to arrive at integration and integrity. When this occurs new and fresh energy boosts our true sense of self, morale, kindness, personal connection, and innovation. Everything we have done before needs re-examination followed by a healthy dose of the creative and connective feminine that's been lacking. As with my own personal story of burn-out and a wake-up call, the earth's warming is a wake-up call for all of us to rediscover, reclaim, and move forward as whole people, as agents of renewal, reinvigorating our lives, our livelihoods, and the systems that make our lives and life on earth possible.

Here are some actions you can take *now* to begin exploring your hero or heroine's journey as an agent of renewal in our global rite of passage. I encourage you to do them all—for yourself and with clients—to see what unfolds. The key to achieving new and solid results is ongoing *practice* that reinforces the results on each step of your journey.

Find a coach, mentor, therapist, or teacher to support you in a deeper and more profound awakening that can open your mind and heart to an expanded view. Ask them to help hold you accountable for walking your talk.

Get out into nature frequently. A few moments, a day or longer stretch of time helps you connect with the wonders of natural beauty wherever you live. Become more attentive to the seasonal shifts around you. Appreciating the sky, sunrise or sunset, the moon and stars can fill you with awe, wonder and gratitude, accelerating your journey to wholeness.

Learn a mindfulness practice as simple as mindful breathing or guided and unguided meditation and visualization. Use yoga, poetry, or sacred writing; dance, singing, or chanting to calm your inner mind-chatter and help you begin to experience greater stillness, balance, and harmony within. When you begin to slow down it will become easier for thoughts to move freely through you leaving more room for a sense of peace, even bliss.

Connect daily to what lights you up—your passion, desire, inner fire, and wild freedom.

Engage in deep listening with others. Ask gentle, open-ended questions to better understand before trying to be understood. For example, "Can you share more about…?" You'll be more effective at this kind of connecting communication if you first fill yourself up by doing some of the above in order to be fully present for others.

Write or journal to enhance your understanding of yourself. People who journal begin to heal and empower themselves more quickly, better understand their thought processes, and become more open to seeing new creative options and solutions. A structured daily journal or any creative practice that supports you to write and process on a regular basis is highly recommended. (Check out my own, *My Life Through the Seasons, A Wisdom Journal and Planner* for this purpose.)

As entrepreneurs serving ourselves, others, and the world it's now essential to explore our own hero's journey instead of blindly following others or reaching for a hollow external reward or artificial sense of success. Know that the more authentic path I invite you to take is not a simple linear one. Like the seasons themselves, it is cyclical and the stages I talk about may not be in sequence. It will look different for you, because you are unique in the world and have unique gifts to contribute. When your own hero's journey becomes more embedded with deep meaning, using creative exploration and finding solutions benefitting others becomes more than a business—it's a sacred trust.

Ask yourself this now: Is it time to begin my journey—for myself, my children, for their children, and our communities?

Own your own inner guidance, listen to the parts of you that may be calling or crying out to be acknowledged. Learn how to integrate the healthy feminine and masculine parts of yourself. When you and I commit to building a reflective practice, opening to nature, deepening our mindfulness practice, and allowing our passions to shine brightly, all those around us share the positive impacts.

We are standing at the precipice, the threshold, together—knowingly or not. Can you find the courage to reach out to another with kindness and compassion, in turn strengthening that part of you? Join me in becoming an agent of renewal, like a lighthouse standing strong, casting a powerful guiding light over the crashing waves, even when—especially when—everything seems to be falling down around us. Our descendants and our planet need you as one among many agents of renewal—a champion of both the practical and the sacred.

As a professional transitions coach, trainer, and author, I am committed to helping people connect to their healthy feminine and healthy masculine in order to experience inner peace and joy again. Often my clients have difficulty sharing their emotions or lack the emotional language and tools to fully explore their inner worlds. I looked everywhere for a structured journal that could clearly guide people on their journeys. Finding none, I was called to develop my own. I created *My Life Through the Seasons, A Wisdom Journal and Planner*, published four times a year, with a different theme for each season. It's a powerful tool for daily and weekly reflection using brain-based research, mindfulness, positive psychology principles, and proven practices. These journals foster connection to one's inner wisdom and intuition supported by the power of nature to build greater emotional resiliency, groundedness, clarity, and everyday joy in living.

***

To contact Karen:

www.seasonalwisdomjournal.com

www.karinlubin.com

linkedin.com/in/dr-karin-lubin

https://www.facebook.com/karin.lubin

email: info@seasonalwisdomjournal.com

# Dr. Tianna Conte

Dr. Tianna Conte is a trailblazing blend of mystic, scientist and international bestselling author of Love's Fire Trilogy and multiple books on transformation. Born with the gift of multi-sensory abilities and various spiritual awakenings including a near- death- experience, Tianna brings an intuitive knowing of human consciousness and life to the entrepreneurial journey. She focuses on training others to live their life with passion, purpose and pleasure.

Her career has spanned forty years as a trained naturopath, ordained interfaith minister, initiated shaman, and psycho-spiritual therapist specializing in energy medicine, enlightened self-care and personal evolution. Integrating ancient wisdom with cutting edge energy psychology has earned her a reputation as a "physician" to the soul.

She is the founder of a signature program, GPS (GodSource Positioning System) Code, in collaboration with her beloved husband, William, in spirit. This ego friendly spiritual system empowers each person to navigate life's challenges in five simple steps that re-awakens one's divine guidance and innate soul powers. This access to silence mind chatter and release reactive emotions show the way to living life to the fullest to enjoy the ride

## Entrepreneurship as a Destiny Driven Life

***By Dr. Tianna Conte***

Are you aware of the moment you decided to embrace the journey of being an entrepreneur? Do you remember what prompted you to make that choice? The reason I ask these questions is because I invite you to explore the possibility that entrepreneurship goes beyond conditioning. I believe that it is a call to a greater awakening and yearning for freedom greater than security and that it stirs from one's soul essence.

Looking back on my life, I can daresay, I have been a forever entrepreneur, tasting of its freedom and fulfillment at an early age. I believe that hidden in our childhood is the seeds of our soul's gifts and that every person has this uniqueness of expression. However, for many people, the outside authorities of parents, school and society instill the need to get a job or even enter a career for fear-based reasons.

This is in sharp contrast to trust your natural talents and intuition to show you the way. The message of follow your heart, do what comes effortlessly and timelessly is lost in the noise of earning a living rather than discover and profit from your destiny. The good news is that it is never too late to pursue your dreams and calling.

I encourage all parents reading this message to watch what your children present as their creative self-expression and encourage that development. I am living proof of the success that this wisdom and support can manifest.

I was born to immigrant parents that came from Italy to pursue their dreams in America. My father was a medical doctor who, together with my traditional housewife mother, raised my sister and I in the little Italy section of the Bronx in New York. He came here with the proverbial clothes on his back.

I witnessed daily how through vision, passion, compassion and tireless work, he provided us with an abundant life. I watched as he loved what he did and how countless people loved him for doing it. The stirrings of my entrepreneurship were awakened through this modelling. The only downside to my father was that he was a workaholic and time with him was precious and rare, except for one day a week.

Enter the destiny of a precocious doctor's daughter. LOL… that would be me. In my quest for time with daddy, I would frequent his office, which was on the second floor of our three-story house. I innocently would visit with his patients who would often wait for hours to see him. Those were the days of no appointments. You just arrived and waited your turn to see the doctor. They would often bring their food, knitting, anything to whittle away the time.

I seized my opportunity to carve out time with my father by trusting my impulses as well as escaping from my emotionally abusive mother. I would go downstairs and introduce myself to his patients and ask permission to lay my hands on their boo boo to make it better. Naturally, all would delight in my antics and respond, yes.

Little did anyone realize I had the gift of what is known as clairvoyance and could see "dark" spots where the energy blockages of their dis-ease were located in their body. All they knew, was they felt better with me and soon started bringing me gifts in appreciation of my handiwork.

However, my sights were on being inside the office where my father worked and not merely remaining in the waiting room. Patience and persistence paid off and soon the opening I had longed for happened. My father had a patient that stymied his ability to diagnose and treat. I believed I could help my father and offered my awareness.

This is the turning point of my journey and a key point for parents to listen carefully to the mere mouthings of a child. By that I mean, my father could have reprimanded my intrusion. Instead, he playfully encouraged me to share my wisdom through the words, "how can you help daddy" with a curious look registered on his face?

I promptly announced, "the man's face is that of a mosquito." My father's light bulb moment happened as he ran out of the room. He returned with a big book and asked me how I could see such a thing. It turned out the man had returned from a safari in Africa and had malaria. My father had never seen nor treated a case of malaria.

Opportunity that I had longed for had finally arisen and my father invited me into his sacred inner office. I was instructed to listen quietly and then we would discuss the cases. I would tell him what I saw and he would share with me what illness they had. I would watch how whatever symptom a patient presented, he would put his hands on that area and encourage the emotional expression of what was related to what was happening in their life. The beginnings of the best training in mind/body healing took roots. I was a mere seven years old!

My father also encouraged a prosperity consciousness that left an imprint for me that I am eager to pass on to all. My father would often be paid in cash and had piles of bills on his desk. One day, my eyes were riveted on the amount of money before me and he addressed me in an empowering way. He turned to me and inquired, "You want to be paid for your time and talent too?" I had never considered such an option and quickly responded, "Yes, thank you!"

Before me were bills ranging from $1.00 to $100.00 and he invited me to take one bill only. Naturally, I reached for the highest bill even though I did not know what to do with it. Innocently, I asked my father to cash it for me. Here were his wise words to me, which when followed, provide a strong foundation for wealth: "Save some, spend some, share some."

As you can tell from reading my story, my father was my hero and mentor. I was on course to have a privileged life when tragedy struck. I was thirteen years when my father died of lung cancer, even though he was a non-smoker. The same day of his funeral, I was sexually violated by a trusted family member under the guise of consoling me on such a devastating loss.

Life, as I was enjoying it, was forever changed. I was thrust into a world of desperation, no support and needing to care for my mentally challenged mother and legally blind sister. No one to turn to for guidance that was safe, I turned to a higher power I referred to as God. First, it was to rail at such a horrible wounding happening to me and then it was to offer God a second chance as my father had taught me to do for all people.

The outcome is what has evolved into my life's purpose and legacy. As I both cursed the divine and welcomed the guidance required to survive, I had my first of many spiritual experiences. The gift of clairaudience burst forth and I heard the words that have sourced my sacred calling: "Surrender each day, step by step, you will be shown the way." These words, decades later, were to become the foundation of my signature program, The GPS Code.

I never gave up on life and pressed on despite the darkness. Many refer to this as the dark night of the soul. I beg to differ and offer another perception. It is the dark night of the ego because I believe the soul has a blueprint for our highest destiny. The ego often does not have a clue and is the part of us that suffers from lack of knowing the bigger picture. It is important to remember that spiritual teachings remind us that life happens through us and not to us.

I relied on trusting this higher power to guide me through the adversity. I can assure you that you have the answers beyond your conscious mind. Learning to quiet the voices and reactive emotions of fear can be the liberating factor and solution you may be seeking.

By doing so, I affectionately claim that I have never had a human being that I have called, my boss. I am probably unemployable as I have only worked for God direct as in self-employed. To me this adventure and trust into the unknown with faith beyond fear is the essence of entrepreneurship.

Aligned with my childhood experiences, I studied pre-med in college and graduated with my degree majoring in biology and psychology. Even though my father had died, I was entering medical school, following in his footsteps.

However, without going into details of yet further tragic turn of events, I left medical school and embarked in an import and export business, traveling the globe. Destiny had once again forged a curious plan beyond my knowing. Regardless of the country, I was introduced to indigenous shamans and healers and the study of altered states of consciousness.

Eventually, I studied in-depth in the healing arts, trained as a naturopath and specialized in mind/body energy psychology. This took place in the eighties when barely anyone in mainstream society understood this work. All to say, trusting guidance and taking risks often bring you into uncharted territory you could have never figured out.

Indeed, my most outrageous entrepreneurial venture was the mood rings. They were to symbolize a biofeedback mechanism for registering stress in the body. However, without being patented correctly, they were marketed as a fad item to indicate if the ring stone turned black, you were frigid and if the ring stone turned blue, you were passionate. This promotion was marketing gold.

I had already garnered success in my private practice. Even with an unlisted phone number and no business cards, it seems true that God works in mysterious ways as I was always fully booked.

I remember waking up in the morning grateful for loving the work I was doing, excited that my clients were transforming their lives and I was prospering beyond belief. Now with the mood rings, this addition further skyrocketed my impact to a level I could never have imagined. All it took was one idea that inspired me that I acted upon.

I willingly divulge this sneak peek and inspired action that catapulted my entrepreneurial journey. Please let this encourage you as a reminder to always follow a positive nudge from the universe. Especially if the risk is minimal, take even a small step outside your comfort zone and let the miracle reveal itself.

This was before the age of the internet. I wrote index cards and placed them in schools and colleges inviting anyone who wanted to earn money for the holidays and be their own boss to contact me for a low risk, high reward opportunity.

I literally had hundreds of people mentoring with me en masse and turning small investments into massive holiday cash. Naturally, I profited to the tune of thousands of dollars on autopilot and the rest is history. Today, this would probably be referred to as rudiments to affiliate and/or network marketing.

I remain ever evolving as an entrepreneur to this day. I laughingly quote as a motto for the boomers of my generation, refire rather than retire! I am passionate in the knowing that if I can follow that still small voice of spirit, you can do it also.

After decades of living this amazing journey of entrepreneurship and investing hundreds of thousands of dollars in my own education and awakening, I am committed to passing on this wisdom through what I refer to as secrets, shortcuts and ego friendly spiritual system.

The secret is best summed up in the quote of Nikola Tesla, "If you want to find the secrets of the universe, think in terms of energy, frequency and vibration."

The shortcut is expressed by my riddle: "What do we all have, regardless of sex, color, socioeconomic etc., that is constantly speaking to us 24 hours 7 days per week and few if any are listening to its communication?" The answer is your body and the shortcut is non-toxic frequency patches of light that puts the power of self-healing into your hands. You can read more on how light therapy stimulates your body's innate healing and regenerating abilities by going to www.shiftandgrowrich.com

As to the system, I offer you The GPS Code for accelerating your soul's destiny driven life. It was spiritually transmitted to me through a series of mystical experiences and is intended to navigate life's challenges in 5 simple steps for accessing your unique soul guidance and superpowers. I offer a complimentary jump start video to set your mornings up for a miracle day go to www.spiritualitymadepractical.com

I trust my story can provide entertainment and enlightenment for you to reflect on how destiny has shaped your life. We can either embrace our wounds or transform the tragedy into triumph. In so doing, we express our soul's potential and become a higher and best version of who we truly are as spiritual beings having a physical experience. The other option is we succumb to being a victim and relegate ourselves to living a limited life.

I daresay, there are no coincidences, accidents or mistakes and in reading this book, what you are searching and deserve is "freedom." You know you want to live a bigger life and deserve more. The lure of having it all is actually our birthright and destiny! This includes freedom physically, emotionally, mentally, spiritually and financially to live life to the fullest. The following are a few key suggestions that can empower and facilitate your personal freedom.

Believe in yourself

The opposite of "believe in yourself" is "self-doubt." When you doubt yourself, you give your power away to doubt. We've all heard those voices in our head saying, "You're not good enough." "You are going to fail." You know the voice I'm talking about. That silent whisper that haunts you when you set a goal to have and become more and you are not sure how to get there. That voice of self-criticism when you hit a stumbling block. When you hear those voices, realize that they are not you. Those voices are past programming, past experiences, trying to keep you where you are, safe a secure.

I have found that the more you fight self-doubt the more it fights back. So, I utilize The GPS Code and/or ask a question. When faced with self-doubt, STOP for a moment and ask yourself if this is really true? Ask yourself "If I proceed with this self-doubt will it help me to accomplish my goal?" Remember self-doubt is fear based. It's a made-up story about some future event that has not, and most likely will not happen. It's not real. Let it go and move on.

I have found that just recognizing that you are experiencing self-doubt and backing away for a moment and seeing it for what it is will weaken the self-doubt. And the more you practice it the more courageous and determined you become.

Follow your passion

As I mentioned, we have been told what to do all our lives by our parents, teachers, professors, religious leaders and employers. When I started deciding for myself what was best for me, my life changed dramatically.

There will always be the critics out there trying to pull you down and crush your dreams. Don't listen. That's their internal dialog, not yours. That's their issues, not yours.

Make your choices and don't be afraid of what others will say. When fear grabs you, see it for what it is. It is not real. Say "Thanks for sharing and that's not me."

Remember fear or any other negative emotion is not hanging onto you, rather you are hanging onto it. It's your choice to hang on or let it go. I have had self-doubt and plenty of it. One day I decided if I wanted more of what life had to offer, I had to believe in myself. I had to face my self-doubt, my fears and be willing to take care of it through making the choices aligned with my values

Look at it this way. Self-doubt is a part of you that's crying for help. It needs understanding. If you want to release self-doubt, I encourage you have to make aligned choices instead of fighting against your doubt. When your choices are in tune with your authentic self, doubt will disappear.

Instead of doubting your abilities and asking yourself "Why? Why am I experiencing this painful situation," ask yourself instead, "What can I do to become better?"

**Break the cycle**

The problem is that people most often go with the obvious. We rely on the same thinking, habits, behaviors and methods that we've used in the past. Go to school, get a degree, get a job, work 40 years and then retire on half of what you couldn't live on while working. That is a outdated model ala.1950's!

Look around you. There are more people choosing entrepreneurship today than ever before. If you prefer a job, that's okay. However, at the same time I caution you to start thinking like an entrepreneur, because that job could be gone tomorrow. Plus if you learn to think like an entrepreneur, you become more valuable to your employer.

Most people are like a fly on the window, trying harder and harder to break through, doing more of the same and getting nowhere fast. We resist new approaches because they make us feel more at risk…more uncomfortable.

However, if you want rich rewards, rapidly, I encourage you to vigorously search out and implement new attitudes and behaviors. The more you are willing to break free of old routines, the greater you will find a better approach. The time is now to re-invent yourself as times change. Are you willing to step up and do something different than what you may be accustomed to?

Reflect? Do you have all the time freedom you want at this point in your life? Do you take the vacations you want every year, or spend quality time with your family? Is your level of financial freedom today where you thought you would be years back? I would urge you to take a realistic look. Are you making progress or coasting downhill? More importantly, what's your plan for the future?

I have found that there are no guarantees in life. However, I do know this: If you want a different result you have to do something in a different.

As I mentioned, I am a committed entrepreneur and a spiritual success mentor. I own two businesses and I wouldn't think of ever doing anything different. In my mentoring practice, I'll show you how to discover and follow your passion, and to do it *your* way aligned with your destiny and soul's calling.

**Invest in yourself**

Ponder this awareness, whatever you have in your life at this very moment is a result of how you see yourself. For example, if you are a person is earning a six-figure income that's how you see yourself. As you change, your experience change. The question becomes, "What do you desire to change about yourself to go from where you are to where you want to be?"

My recommendation is to take a step… hire a coach, read uplifting and informative books, listen to personal development audios, attend seminars, etc. Learning, growing and making better choices aligned with my values have been the catalyst for me.

Especially since The GPS Code uses car analogy, I invite you to consider this perception. When something goes wrong with your automobile you take it to the repair shop, right? Top performers have coaches and mentors. Where do *you* go when you need a check up on your own performance?

Just like a 3,000 mile check-up on your automobile, consider this idea, periodically conduct your own performance self-evaluation. Ask yourself, "How am I really doing? Am I doing all I can? Am I making full use of my talents? Am I working on myself and developing the skills to go to the next level of performance?" Am I just "cruising" along and maintaining "status quo" while blaming others or outside circumstances for my lack of performance? Am I living up to my full potential?" And I urge you to answer these questions and others as objectively as possible.

Clue, if you don't pass your check-up, seek support immediately. You deserve to have the best life possible and a mentor may be your pathway.

**Status Quo**

This may come as a shock to you; complacency and coasting in the comfort zone is seductive. Many people would much rather just maintain the status quo. They spend the majority of their time focused on and complaining about what they *don't have* and focused on what they *don't want*, instead of focusing on what they *do want* in their lives.

I know that's not you, because you are reading this book. You know that if you want change, you have to take action to change. A few closing tips:

**Clarify what is it that you want?** What end result are you striving for…and more importantly, Why? What will this objective provide to you? Why you want it will be the driving force

**Create aligned steps of action.** What could you do to today that would take you closer to your dreams? Keep moving forward. Even small steps can make a big difference.

**Don't give up**. If you meet with challenges that get you down. Get up and dust yourself off and focus on your vision and mission. You can do it. Keep moving forward.

**Make a commitment to yourself.** Make a commitment that doesn't allow for anything less. A commitment is a promise you make to yourself that you will not stop until your dream is realized.

**Need help? Ask for it.** You deserve the best and do not need to go for it alone. If you find you are overwhelmed and don't know where to turn, ask for help. Hiring a coach or mentor is a good place to start. I'm here to empower you and guide you in trusting your innate wisdom. I would love to work with you!

PS- Let's talk! As I shared earlier in this chapter, I love to get to know each person I meet and discover how best I can be of support. You are unique and so is your journey.

***

To Contact Dr. Tianna:

Telephone 1-914-205-4969

Email: drtianna@gmail.com

www.drtianna.com

www.yourgpscode.com

www.facebook.com/tianna.conte.77

www.facebook.com/gpscode

www.linkedin.com/in/drtianna

www.twitter.com/drtianna

#1 Best-Selling Co-Author Love's Fire series

Intimate true and transformational

Love story of evolutionary possibilities

www.loves-fire.com

Founder, GPS Code, for navigating life's challenges

in 5 simple steps for accessing soul's guidance & power

www.yourgpscode.com

Producer and Co-Star documentary

inspired by Think and Grow Rich, Awaken Your Riches

www.movieandmastermind.com

(Free VIP gifts for love, wellness and

wealth......Access all and Enjoy)

www.infinitepossibilitiesproductions.com

# Afterword

Life and business are always a series of transitions… people, places, and things that shape who we are as individuals. Often, you never know that the next catalyst for improving your business and life is around the corner, in the next person you meet or the next book you read.

Jim Britt and Kevin Harrington have spent decades influencing individuals and entrepreneurs with strategies to grow their business, developing the right mindset and mental toughness to thrive in today's business environment and to live a better life.

Allow all you have read in this book to create a new you, to reinvent yourself and your business model if required, because every business and life level requires a different you. It's your journey to craft.

*Cracking the Rich Code* is a series that offers much more than a book. It's a community of like-minded influencers from around the world. A global movement. Each chapter is like opening a surprise gift, that just may contain the one idea that changes everything for you. Watch for future releases and add them to your collection. If you know of anyone who would like to be considered as a co-author for a future volume, have them email our offices at support@jimbritt.com

The individual and combined works of Jim Britt and Kevin Harrington have filled seminar rooms to maximum capacity and created a worldwide demand. If you get the opportunity to attend one of their live events, jump at the chance. You'll be glad you did.

If you are a coach, speaker, consultant of entrepreneur and would like to get the details about becoming a coauthor in the next Cracking the Rich Code book in the series, contact Jim Britt at jimbritt@jimbritt.com.

To Schedule Jim Britt or Kevin Harrington as a featured speaker at your next convention or special event, email: support@jimbritt.com

Master your moment as they become hours that become days.

Make it a great life!

Your legacy awaits.

STAY IN TOUCH WITH JIM AND KEVIN

For daily strategies and insights from top entrepreneurs, join us at

THE RICH CODE CLUB

**FREE** members site.

www.TheRichCodeClub.com

www.ingramcontent.com/pod-product-compliance
Lightning Source LLC
Chambersburg PA
CBHW071204210326
41597CB00016B/1663